Origin and Role of the European Bank for Reconstruction and Development

Origin and Role of the European Bank for Reconstruction and Development

Paul A. Menkveld

Graham & Trotman

A member of Wolters Kluwer Academic Publishers

LONDON/DORDRECHT/BOSTON

Graham & Trotman Ltd.
Sterling House
66 Wilton Road
London SW1V 1DE

Kluwer Academic Publishers Group
101 Philip Drive
Assinippi Park
Norwell, MA 02061 USA

British Library Cataloguing in Publication Data

Menkveld, Paul A.
  Origin and role of the European Bank for
  Reconstruction and Development.
  I. Title
  332.15

  ISBN 1-85333-626-2

Library of Congress Cataloging-in-Publication Data

Menkveld, Paul A.
  Origin and role of the European Bank for Reconstruction and
  Development / Paul A. Menkveld.
      p.   cm.
  Includes bibliographical references and index.
  ISBN 1-85333-626-2
  1. European Bank for Reconstruction and Development. 2. Europe,
  Eastern—Economic conditions—1989-   I. Title.
  HG3881.5.E83M46   1991
  332.1'53—dc20   91-30744
                                                      CIP

Typeset in ITC Garamond by BookEns Ltd, Baldock, Herts.
Printed and bound in Great Britain by Hartnolls Ltd, Bodmin, Cornwall

Contents

Preface

The European Bank for Reconstruction and Development had a stormy conception and a controversial birth. Doubts were expressed about its purpose, its scope, its location and its leadership almost from the beginning. The time from conception in or around November 1989 to its opening in the spring of 1991 was remarkably short for an institution of such complexity. Its reception and the reception of its president Jacques Attali in the Anglo-Saxon and German press has been less than adulatory.

Some of this reflects—no doubt—political objections to the provenance of this original idea in the French administration. Most of the opposition however is based on genuine concern about how a new institution can contribute to the extraordinarily complex process of transformation going on in the post-communist societies of East and Central Europe and in the Soviet Union.

In such circumstances critical commentaries on the EBRD cannot be dismissed simply as effusions of the 'not-invented-here' syndrome. To understand therefore the potential purpose of the EBRD requires a careful discussion of its conception and birth. This is what Paul Menkveld has set out to do.

By the end of this book the reader will have a clear idea of the many twists and turns in the negotiations to set up the bank. How it moved from a purely European concept to include OECD members and beyond. How the remit moved from a rather traditional development bank to an institution which could lend no more than 40% of its funds to the public sector and which consequently has to have a high-powered merchant banking department rather than the more usual raft of social cost-benefit analysts.

The reader will also begin to grasp the importance of the explicit political conditionality in the EBRD charter. In this it is at its closest to being a unique institution. Other institutions have explicit conditionality in their dealings with East and Central Europe—notably the European Investment Bank. The EBRD however approaches the width of membership of the Bretton Woods institutions whereas the EIB is EC members only. Equally there have been occasions where the IMF or the World Bank have suspended action as a result of political events—Tianamen Square for example. But these institutions have rules explicitly against political criteria for involvement—hence the membership of many countries which would not meet the criteria of democracy and the market economy set by the EBRD.

The question of conditionality is likely to be one of the most difficult for the EBRD. In circumstances where everyone is learning by doing mistakes are inevitable. Democracy and the market economies are like elephants in being difficult to define. Everyone however is sure they can recognise them when they see them. Not every one unfortunately has the same animal in mind. The management of that problem along with the more mundane but no less important task of using a public sector organisation—with the inevitably heavy mechanisms of account-ability—to pursue private sector development while maintaining a high credit rating when lending to risky ventures is the key challenge for the EBRD in the 1990s.

Paul Menkveld's book by clarifying the genesis of the EBRD will help those interested to judge the EBRD's performance over the coming decade.

J.M.C. Rollo
Head, International Economics Programme
Royal Institute of International Affairs
July 1991

Acknowledgments

Under the FCO Scholarship Awards Scheme the Dutch Ministry of Foreign Affairs offered me sabbatical leave in London for the academic year 1990-1991. Through the kind offices of the British Embassy in The Hague and the Amsterdam office of the British Council, arrangements were made for my attachment as a research scholar to the London School of Economics and Political Science and as a visiting fellow of the Royal Institute of International Affairs at Chatham House. My research activities concentrated on the origin and role of the newly established European Bank for Reconstruction and Development.

I should like to thank all of those who, in different ways, have contributed to make the sabbatical year possible and who advised on the preparations of this book. I particularly want to acknowledge the assistance of Jim Rollo of Chatham House and Chris Willcox of the London School of Economics. Furthermore I have benefited from a number of interviews conducted in various European Community capitals and financial centres, as well as from a study group meeting on the text of the manuscript, organised by the Royal Institute of International Affairs at Chatham House. Needless to say, however, the views expressed in this book are my responsibility, as are any mistakes or omissions.

Paul A. Menkveld
London, July 1991

List of Abbreviations

ACP	African, Caribbean and Pacific countries
ADB	Asian Development Bank
AfDB	African Development Bank
CMEA	Council for Mutual Economic Assistance
CSCE	Conference on Security and Co-operation in Europe
EBRD	European Bank for Reconstruction and Development
EC	European Community
ECSC	European Coal and Steel Community
ECU	European Currency Unit
EIB	European Investment Bank
EFTA	European Free Trade Association
G-7	Group of 7
G-24	Group of 24
GATT	General Agreement on Tariffs and Trade
GDR	German Democratic Republic
IADB	Inter-American Development Bank
IBRD	International Bank for Reconstruction and Development
IFC	International Finance Corporation
IGO	International Governmental Organisation
IIB	International Investment Bank
IMF	International Monetary Fund
NATO	North Atlantic Treaty Organisation
OECD	Organisation for Economic Co-operation and Development
PHARE	Poland/Hungary Aid for Economic Restructuring programme

Chapter One

Introduction

This is a survey of the European Bank for Reconstruction and Development, an intergovernmental organisation recently established to channel Western financial resources and technical assistance to the transforming economies of reforming states and societies in Central and Eastern Europe. Opinions on the geographical labelling of the Soviet Union differ. In this book, as in the EBRD Agreement, the Soviet Union forms part of Central and Eastern Europe. The purpose of this survey is to focus upon the period October 1989 to April 1991, i.e. the period starting with the launching of the initiative to establish a development/investment bank to assist countries in Central and Eastern Europe in their transition towards more market-oriented economies and ending at the time when the European Bank for Reconstruction and Development, which evolved out of this initiative, became operational.

In both the reform process and the creation of a new institution, the initiators, the Soviet Union and France, were soon joined by more decisive partners. The 'new thinking' in Soviet foreign policy in the last part of the 1980s together with the collapse of the economies of the centrally planned countries paved the way for other Central and Eastern European countries to pursue their own paths. This freedom of choice led to the collapse of a number of Communist regimes and the introduction of drastic economic reform policies in former Soviet satellites. Changes that by far surpassed expectations, put the reform policy in the Soviet Union itself in the shade. France, wanting to assist not only the

reform front-runners but also the 'new thinking' Soviet Union
regime as well, turned to 'old thinking' and launched another of
its rather bold political initiatives. The establishment of a 'Bank
for Europe', bringing Europe together in a development/invest-
ment bank type of institution to finance major projects in Central
and Eastern Europe. France did succeed in convincing its European Community partners to accept the idea. The EBRD, however,
did not emerge as a traditional regional development/investment
bank. During the mandate negotiations the original French idea
evolved into the creation of a different kind of institution. The
original idea, the negotiations and the mandate of this new kind
of institution form the core of this survey.

The initiative to create a new intergovernmental organisation
with membership across the Iron Curtain was triggered by the
political events in the region east of this demarcation line.
Therefore chapter 2 begins with a summary of the political and
economic context at the time of the French initiative. The chapter
considers what happened in Central and Eastern Europe in the
second half of 1989, the period that started with free elections
in Poland and ended with the fall of the Berlin Wall and the execution of Romania's dictator; a period in which the Soviet leader
Mr. Gorbachev was still surrounded by reformers. After a brief
review of the main political events, attention turns to economics;
the economic recipe to transform centrally planned economies
into more market-oriented economies. The recommendations
centred around macro economic stabilisation, economic liberalisation and mass privatisation. One of the reform results was
that, in general, the East changed its policy of independence
into a relationship of preferably interdependence with and if
necessary dependence upon the West. The last section of this
chapter therefore deals with the Western response. What could
the West do and what did the West do in 1989? For co-ordinated bilateral assistance, the carrot and stick method was
adopted. Substantial assistance was made available only for the
front-runners in reform. Commitment to reform was not sufficient. For the existing multilateral organisations on the other
hand it was business as usual, that is to say the issue of political
orientation did not play a role.

Having described the framework chapter 3 turns to the EBRD
concept. What was the original idea, what were the objectives
and how was the initiative launched? The French announced

that they had in mind an institution similar to the European Investment Bank. Therefore the purpose and functions of this development/investment bank are investigated in some detail and attention paid to the phenomena of international institutions in more general terms. Next the French motives are reviewed, the publicly stated ones and very likely others as well. In the first category, assistance to the Soviet Union plays the leading role; in the second category French *gloire*. In the light of this, the question of whether a new institution was necessary to fulfil the French objectives is looked at. This includes the scrutiny of possible alternatives such as the International Finance Corporation and the European Investment Bank. Not surprisingly pros and cons can be seen. But this issue becomes hypothetical as France succeeds in convincing its European Community partners to accept the idea of establishing a new institution. Although it was agreed that the new institution should have a basically European character the Community favoured membership by all OECD countries and beyond.

Chapter 4 turns to the negotiations during the constitutive conference. France, keeping the momentum alive, organised and chaired the meetings. The first section of this chapter deals with the participants and conference procedures. Why did Third World countries want to become members of the new institution, and so make financial contributions to the, generally speaking, less poor Second World. Solidarity, procurement, political reasons? A choice had to be made between a mandate similar to those of existing development/investment banks, the French concept, and a mandate based on political conditions, a concept encouraged by, among others, the United States, along with a restricted recipient status for the Soviet Union. Although the United States wanted Western Europe to lead the overall Western assistance towards the smaller countries of Central and Eastern Europe, they kept dictating the rules of the game, in good hegemonic tradition, as far as the Soviet Union's role was concerned. In past decades this had prevented the superpowers from working together in international financial institutions. But times have changed. Now both the Soviet Union and the United States wanted to stay aboard, albeit with the United States replacing France as captain of the ship and the Soviet Union, on the other hand, becoming an unpaid crew member. Then the difficult details such as the size of the capital stock, division of shares and voting power needed to be dealt with. And last but not least the issue of the presidency and the city to host the headquarters had to be agreed. In this context the European G-7 countries staged a fine piece of theatre leaving the smaller European Community members states, some muttering objections, empty-handed.

In chapter 5 the EBRD Agreement, a document containing 63 articles, is summarised, focusing on the mandate and the structure of the bank. In the mandate section attention will be paid to the purpose, functions and resources of the bank. The purpose and functions of this new institution are spelled out in detail in its charter. This might have been caused by the concern to keep the bank's operations in line with its overall political and economic orientation. A review of the structure of the bank follows, explaining its familiar three tier set up, with a Board of Governors, Board of Directors and the bank's management and staff. Compared to the size of its capital and number of shareholders the number of Directors appointed by the shareholders (23) is impressive. The last section of this chapter deals with membership of the EBRD, membership of the countries and institutions that signed the Agreement in May 1990 and the way in which other countries can join the bank at a later stage.

In chapter 6 the preparatory phase, the period from the signing of the Agreement in May 1990 up to April 1991, the month in which the bank became operational is looked at. The two monthly follow-up conferences dealing with by-laws, rules of procedure, the organisational structure of the bank and staff matters are examined. Special attention is paid to the issue of the appointment of Vice-Presidents and the draft plan of operations. The chapter ends with the inaugural ceremony, held in London on 15 April 1991. Elements of various keynote addresses are highlighted, covering the origin and role of the EBRD from different perspectives.

In the final, summarizing chapter, chapter 7, the emergence of the EBRD is looked at in retrospect as well as in perspective. First, the original idea is compared to the outcome of the negotiations, indicating how and under whose influence the original concept evolved during the process. Then the question is raised as to which problems the new institution will be able to address in the context of the overall challenge that the countries in Central and Eastern Europe face in their transition towards market-oriented economies, and on which activities the bank should concentrate in order to use its facilities to the greatest benefit of the countries in Central and Eastern Europe. Finally, the widely varying opinions on the need to create the EBRD and on the role the bank can play are examined.

Chapter Two

The Political and Economic Context

The purpose of the European Bank for Reconstruction and Development is 'to foster the transition towards open market-oriented economies and to promote private and entrepreneurial initiative in the Central and Eastern European countries committed to and applying the principles of multiparty democracy, pluralism and market economics'.[1] The establishment of this new international financial institution was the result of a French initiative, launched in the autumn of 1989. For a proper evaluation of the origin and the role of the EBRD, the relevant political and economic context at the time of the initiative should be looked into. This will be the theme of this chapter. First, attention will be paid to some of the main political events in Central and Eastern Europe in 1989. In the subsequent section the economic reform requirements for transition of centrally planned economies into market-oriented economies will be highlighted. Finally, attention will be paid to the issue of Western assistance and, in particular, the commitments made in 1989.

2.1 Central and Eastern Europe in 1989

In order to assess the political and economic events in Central and Eastern Europe in 1989 that led to the demolition of the Iron Curtain one has to recall why this Curtain was there in the first place and what it produced. The creation of a separate Eastern political and economic system after the Second World War was a product of the Soviet Union's dominance in Central and Eastern Europe and its international political strategy. According to Marxist ideology the formation of a separate economic bloc would deepen the crisis of world capitalism and speed its inevitable demise.[2] The economic relationship between the capitalist countries of the West and the communist countries of the East became one of independence and confrontation. Both sides established separate international political and economic systems with separate institutions, rules, and patterns of interaction; hence the reference to the dividing Iron Curtain.

Just as there is variety in market-oriented economies, so the centrally planned economies differ one from another. However, the common feature of the centrally planned economies of Central and Eastern Europe is the substantial degree of state ownership of the factors of production[3] and the subordination of economic rationality to political demands. The Communist Party in these countries took over the organisational and disciplinary role of the market in virtually all sectors of the economy. This resulted in centralised resource allocation, monopolistic production structures, autarchic trade policy, non-convertible currencies and a widespread use of subsidies. Over the years this led, compared to market-oriented economies, to distortion of prices, services, labour and capital. Although favouring income equality as well as job security and full employment the centrally planned system proved to be a regime that discouraged innovation, productivity and product quality.

Problems arose in both the agricultural and industrial sector, and the absence of a developed service sector hampered specialisation. The Eastern bloc growth rates declined from an average of 6% per year in the 1950s to about 1–2% by the early 1980s. The average income per head of the population stagnated or declined. Even worse, a large proportion of the income available could not be spent as many consumer goods were not sufficiently available in the shops and markets. Consumers had to spend a great deal of time and energy searching out and queuing for basic goods. An inefficient use of time, to say the least.

The environment suffered badly from the emphasis on energy-intensive heavy industry and a wasteful system of production, due to artificially low energy prices, the fact the polluters were not held responsible and the repression on public opinion. The countries in Central and Eastern Europe are estimated to consume considerably more energy per unit gross domestic product as the industrialised Western countries. The extensive use of brown coal, of which Central and Eastern Europe produces approximately 60% of the world production, has further contributed to the environmental degradation.

The centrally planned economic system was in need of drastic, overall economic reform. Past attempts to adjust the centrally planned system in Central and Eastern Europe without accompanying political reform had not proved successful. The introduction of overall economic reforms in centrally planned states therefore cannot succeed without simultaneous drastic political reform. Transition towards market-oriented economies requires more than extensive personnel changes throughout the Communist Party apparatus. A decisive government policy committed to the principles of political and economic reform, enjoying the support of the population, is needed. It could be expected that sooner or later the kind of sweeping popular movement seen in Hungary in 1956, Czechoslovakia in 1968 and Poland in 1980 would re-emerge.[4] This happened in the course of 1989. The Iron Curtain, which had been rusting for more than a decade, began cracking in places. Poland and Hungary took the lead in implementing political and economic reforms.

In February 1989 round-table negotiations were arranged in Poland between the government, Solidarity and the Catholic Church.[5] An agreement was reached which included the legalisation of the trade union Solidarity, headed by Mr. Lech Walesa, and elections to be held in June 1989. Solidarity did very well in these elections winning 92 of the 100 Senate seats outright, and all but one of the 161 seats that they were allowed to contest out of the 460 Lower House seats. After General Kiszczak, the Interior Minister who had played an important role in the round-table negotiations, proved unable to form a government President Jaruzelski authorised Solidarity to form a majority non-communist government in August 1989. The first non-communist government in post-1948 Central and Eastern Europe. The Solidarity government under Mr. Tadeusz Mazowiecki inherited an economy burdened by an enormous debt problem, with accompanying shortages of foreign exchange, slow growth, accelerating inflation and shortages of basic goods; an economy heading for total collapse.

In Hungary the Hungarian Socialist Workers' Party used its

leading role to promote reforms, not only in the economy but also in the political field. A particularly energetic reformist faction developed around Mr. Imre Pozsgay. This group became embroiled in a power struggle with another, more conservative and authoritarian faction led by General Secretary Karoly Grosz, which the reformers won by the summer of 1989. The power of General Secretary Grosz was considerably reduced through a reshuffling of the leadership of the Party. Furthermore it was decided that a thorough reform of the Party itself was essential. In October 1989 the Hungarian Parliament approved the constitutional amendments agreed in the summer negotiations. Parliamentary elections were to be held in 1990.

In Czechoslovakia the non-communist organisation Civic Forum, combining numerous small opposition groups, emerged rapidly in 1989. The communist power collapsed after a series of massive popular demonstrations in November 1989. The Communist Party leadership under Mr. Milos Jakes failed to secure the support of the Central Committee for repressing the wave of demonstrations and stepped down. Prime Minister Ladislav Adamec recognised the unavoidability of round-table discussions with the opposition and promised to form a new government containing non-communists. After a renewed wave of massive public demonstrations and the threat of a general strike Mr. Adamec was forced to quit. Another government, approved by the opposition, was formed.

In the German Democratic Republic the situation for the Communist Party became unstable after Hungary opened its border to Austria in the summer of 1989, leading to massive emigration of GDR citizens to West Germany. As the migration built up, so did the internal protest. Demonstrations were attended by more and more people. On 18 October 1989 Mr. Erich Honecker, the East German leader since 1971, resigned. He was replaced by his Party colleague Mr. Egon Krenz. Concessions by the regime followed (the Berlin Wall was opened on 9 November 1989). But these proved to be too little and too late. Mr. Krenz and his Politbureau colleagues resigned in December 1989.

In contrast with past conduct, the Soviet Union had made it clear that the solutions to the problems of the other Central and Eastern European countries would not come from Moscow. They could and should pursue their own paths.[6] This freedom of policy was a result of Mr. Gorbachev's reform policies, which gained momentum in the second half of 1989. Mr. Gorbachev addressed economic and political problems differently from his predecessors. Under his domestic political policy known as *glasnost* he took steps towards a greater democratisation of the political process. In the economic field he announced a policy known as *perestroika*, or transformation of the Soviet economy. *Perestroika* also has an international dimension, the improvement of trade and financial interaction with the West in order to speed up the restructuring process.

All in all, the growing problems of the Eastern economic system leading to worn out economies, the policy change in the Soviet Union and the easing of political tensions emerged as forces encouraging the East to end its isolation from the West. But the legacy of economic distortions will not be overcome easily. The best obtainable result is a steady, reliable increase in the standard of living. Even if there is rapid implementation of an overall economic reform policy it will take the countries in Central and Eastern Europe many years to reach the standard of living of even the economically less advanced countries in Western Europe.

2.2 Economic reform requirements

As described in the preceding section, 1989 was a year of drastic political changes in Central and Eastern Europe. A year in the course of which an increasing number of countries in that region moved decisively towards democracy and the implementation of economic reform. The latter involving the transition of centrally planned economies into market-oriented economies. The question was which package of economic reform measures would be required and what should be the magnitude of the various measures? Should reform measures be implemented as rapidly as possible or should the transition be gradual? In what sequence should the various measures be implemented? All these questions arose because of the lack of an empirically tested economic recipe for substituting a market-oriented economy for a centrally planned economy. As a Russian wirter had put it: 'We know that you can turn an aquarium into fish soup; the problem is how to turn fish soup back into an aquarium'.[7]

A substantial number of books, reports, papers and articles

dealing with the transition process were published in 1989, highlighting economic reform measures, emphasising different priorities, pointing out various constraints and recommending a variety of policy menus. One such policy menu was presented by the International Monetary Fund in its paper 'Market-Oriented Reform in Planned Economies' in October 1989.[8] The IMF listed the following elements of market-oriented reform:

1 Reform of the system of micro-economic decision making
   (a) Enterprise autonomy, incentives and financial discipline
   (b) Property rights
   (c) Promotion of competition
2 Price reform
3 Reform of the foreign trade and exchange rate systems
   (a) The organisation and conduct of foreign trade
   (b) The exchange rate system, export incentives, and the allocation of foreign exchange
4 Wage reform and labour market policies
5 Macro-economic management
   (a) Fiscal reform
   (b) Financial sector reform
6 Agricultural reform.

These elements can be combined in three main reform tasks: macro economic stabilisation, economic liberalisation and mass privatisation. Macro economic stabilisation is needed to crack (hyper) inflation and to prevent huge government budget deficits. Furthermore it is necessary to enforce wage restraints and to adjust the balance of payments. To be able to implement a macro economic reform programme reform of the monetary system in Central and Eastern Europe is an essential prerequisite. Such a reform involves the establishment of an independent central bank[9] and of a sound commercial banking system.[10] Although limited, there are some examples of successful implementation of macro economic stablisation programmes in non-OECD countries, e.g. Bolivia and Mexico.

The second main reform task, economic liberalisation, consists of measures like the abolition of central planning, decentralisation of the decision-making authority from state level to enterprise level, the introduction of a legal structure that makes it possible to own and to transfer property, and that guarantees contracts and promotes competition in the domes-

would put severe economic and social pressure on the population: unemployment, a reduction in purchasing power, continuation (at least in the short run) of the scarcity of consumer goods, to mention just a few elements. The success of the economic reform programmes depends on internal factors like political acceptance and social tolerance as well as external factors, such as increased trade opportunities and, last but not least, substantive Western assistance.

2.3 Western assistance committed in 1989

After examining some of the main political events in Central and Eastern Europe in 1989 and economic reform requirements, we turn to the Western response to the political and economic transformations. What kind of economic assistance should the West offer and what level of official assistance would be appropriate? The options for assistance, containing both trade and aid elements, include among others:

- Integration of Central and Eastern Europe in the world economy by
  (a) endorsing membership of these countries of the existing international institutions such as IMF and World Bank and the GATT trade organisation,
  (b) opening up the Western markets for exports of goods, services and labour;
- Short-term balance of payments support and substantive debt relief;
- Knowledge transfer by means of training, technical assistance, technology transfer, institution building and policy advice;
- Support for the private sector.

However, the first question is whether the countries in Central and Eastern Europe were interested in Western assistance? Yes, they were![14] In particular, the 1989 transition front-runners Poland and Hungary were eagerly looking for advice, knowledge transfer, export markets and financial assistance. The next question is whether the West was willing to help. What was the general opinion in the West in the autumn of 1989? The West wished to encourage the changes in the East towards democracy and market-oriented economies, which they saw as being to the benefit of the people living in Central and Eastern Europe and to the benefit of security and stability in Europe as a whole. Furthermore, successful transformation in the East would boost trade opportunities. But as far as aid was concerned the East should be serious about their new policies, not only in rhetoric but also in practice. As Timothy Garton Ash put it accurately: 'Western democracies do have a moral obligation to help, and, what is more, they have a hard political interest in helping the man while he is struggling in the water. Provided, of course, he is really trying to swim, and not just shouting about swimming'.[15] Assistance yes, but conditional, was the general opinion at the time.

The private sector is one of the key targets for assistance. One way of supporting the emerging private sector in Central and Eastern Europe is to make foreign capital available. This can be done on commercial or concessional terms. Who are the potential suppliers of this foreign capital? First, funds can be raised in the international capital markets. However, Poland and to a lesser extent Hungary are already heavily in debt and according to international standards their debt service capacity is considered to be very weak.[16] In contrast to the 1970s private capital does not flow easily to problem debtors now.[17]

Then there is the counterpart private sector in the West, which could make available trade credits and could invest in joint ventures. Analysing the assistance for Poland and Hungary the United Nations Economic Commission for Europe concluded that greater direct investment by Western enterprises is needed if the transforming countries are to develop effective export capacities and achieve real economic growth.[18] Western companies are investing in Central and Eastern Europe, but only on a modest scale. The Western private sector has no moral obligation to grant credit or invest in Central and Eastern Europe. Business requires profit potential, investment security, profit transfers, non-discriminatory tax-laws etc. Governments can help by means of credit insurance, taxation agreements and investment protection agreements.

The Western governments also can make available foreign capital for the private sector in Central and Eastern Europe themselves by loans or grants to the private sector in the countries concerned (to be spent in a mutually agreed way) as well as by means of channelling funds through international financial institutions.

What level of official assistance would be appropriate? What would be the starting point? Reference was occasionally made to the level of US Marshall Aid to Europe in the late 1940s and early 1950s. During the three-and-a-half years of the Marshall Aid the United States transferred 1.3% of its Gross Domestic Product, on average, annually. Using the same percentage, the economies of Western Europe alone could produce more than US $200 billion a year for aid to Central and Eastern Europe.[19] Should the starting point be the absorption capacity of the recipient countries or would an ad hoc approach, at least in the short run, be more suitable given the uncertainties? Preference was given to a flexible ad hoc approach.

Which support measures did the West take or announce in 1989? A whole variety, ranging from trade agreements, trade credits, loans, food aid, aid for economic restructuring and establishment of a stabilisation fund for the Polish currency, to multilateral financial assistance. The assistance was, in particular, geared at the two countries leading in the economic transformation process, Poland and Hungary. For both political and economic reasons Western Europe took the lead and the United States and Japan followed.[20] The Western economic summit in Paris in July 1989 decided to establish a special programme of the Group of 24 (the OECD countries being the 12 EC and 6 EFTA countries and Canada, United States, Australia, New Zealand, Japan and Turkey) to encourage the process of the structural reform in the economies of Poland and Hungary and asked the European Commission to co-ordinate it; the Poland/Hungary Aid for Economic Restructuring (PHARE) programme. The programme covers five main areas: food aid and agricultural restructuring, access to Western markets, investment promotion, professional training and co-operation on environmental problems. In December 1989 this programme was extended to Czechoslovakia, Bulgaria and the German Democratic Republic.[21] Unlike Romania these countries were considered to have made sufficient progress in the political and economic transformation process. A unanimous position regarding the Soviet Union could not be reached.

The European Community concluded a trade and co-operation agreement with Hungary in September 1988 and with Poland's new democratically elected government in September 1989 and the two countries were included in the EC's General

Scheme of Preferences. Under this scheme for developing countries, duties on industrial exports to the Community are abolished and the tariffs on certain agricultural products reduced substantially, although in specific areas quota's will reduce the advantages of tariff reductions. Beyond that negotiations are planned to examine possible forms of association, which might, eventually lead to full membership of the European Community. At the end of 1989 new trade credit for Poland totalled US $2.8 billion (of which West Germany supplied more than half) and for Hungary US $0.7 billion. Bilateral grants, notably for Poland and Hungary, totalled US $1.2 billion.[22]

In October 1989 the US Congress approved a three year aid package of US $852 million for Poland and US $86 million for Hungary, comprising grants to stimulate the private sector, a contribution to the international fund for stabilisation of the Polish currency and emergency food aid.[23] Japan followed with a similar aid package, totallling US $210 million.[24]

The international financial institutions played an important role as well. The IMF arranged stand-by agreements with Poland (US $700 million), Hungary (US $210 million) and Yugoslavia (US $600 million). The World Bank provided loans to Poland (US $360 million) and Hungary (US $1977 million). The international financial institution directing its activities primarily at the private sector, the International Finance Corporation (a World Bank affiliate), made equity investment and loans available for Poland (US $44.4 million), Hungary (US $43.6 million) and Yugoslavia (US $338 million). And the European Investment Bank made an ECU[25] 1000 million facility available for Poland and Hungary.[26]

Chapter Three

The EBRD Concept

Chapter 2 focused on the political and economic context in which the initiative to establish the European Bank for Reconstruction and Development was launched. A brief review of some of the main events in Central and Eastern Europe in 1989 leading towards democracy and economic reform was followed by an overview of economic reform requirements and a summary of the assistance committed by the West to Central and Eastern Europe in 1989. Support for privatisation of public sector enterprises and for the newly emerging private sector enterprises formed an essential part of the Western economic assistance for the process of transforming centrally planned economies into more market-oriented economies. To implement this kind of support a whole range of existing bilateral and multilateral channels was available and virtually all of these channels were subsequently used.

Additionally, an initiative to establish a new multilateral channel to foster foreign direct investment in Central and Eastern Europe was launched in 1989. This French initiative evolved in an agreement to establish the European Bank for Reconstruction and Development, which can be characterised as a new kind of institution. The origin and the character of the EBRD will be the subject of this chapter. First, the underlying idea and the way in which the initiative was launched will be described. Subsequently, attention will be paid to the French motives behind the initiative. Apart from those made public, others not explicitly mentioned, but nevertheless likely will be explored. Then the question of whether the creation of a new, additional support channel, to foster direct foreign investment in Central and Eastern Europe, was necessary to fulfil the envisaged objectives will be discussed. Finally, circumstances that might have influenced the European Community member countries to endorse the French EBRD initiative will be described.

3.1 The French initiative

The idea to establish a 'Bank for Europe'

The idea to establish a new, additional international institution to assist Central and Eastern European countries in the transition of their centrally planned economies towards open market-oriented economies is said to be an idea of Mr. Jacques Attali, special adviser to France's President Mitterrand. Darell Delamaide in an article in Euromoney gave the following background information on Mr. Attali: 'Attali is famous as an ideas man. 'Bubbling' is the word usually used to describe his production of ideas . . . 'He is extraordinarily imaginative and creative' claims a colleague. . . .François Mitterrand has often testified that this intellectual fecundity is one of Attali's most valuable traits as an adviser, even if the ideas require considerable sifting. 'After all', Mitterrand told one interviewer, 'it's enough if Attali gives me one good idea among the 10 he presents to me: that's already quite formidable' . . . Attali says he first thought of the project in August 1989. He said 'it was an obvious idea, an obvious need'.[1]

Obviously President Mitterrand approved of this idea since he made the idea public and subsequently gave it his full political backing. President Mitterrand launched the initiative in a speech before the European Parliament in Strasbourg, which he, in his capacity as President-in-office of the European Council of Heads of State and Government, addressed on 25 October 1989. In an extensive tour d'horizon the President paid considerable attention to the recent events and ongoing developments in Central and Eastern Europe.[2]

In the context of the European response to the needs of the East President Mitterrand stated:[3] 'Poland, Hungary, the Soviet Union and, in his historic leading role, Mr. Gorbachev, need to be helped. . . . Then come large-scale priority projects in fields such as agriculture, transport, telephones and finance. What financing? For my country I have been thinking of a Franco-Polish investment promotion centre . . . with joint banks operating along similar lines. What can Europe do? So much more! Why not set up a Bank for Europe which, like the European Investment Bank, would finance major projects and have on its Board of Directors the 12 European countries. Not to mention the others, such as Poland and Hungary, and why not the Soviet Union, and yet others? It was done for technology and for the audiovisual field under Eureka, so what is holding us back? . . . The creation of a Bank for Europe is a highly political decision.'

Without questioning the originality of Mr. Attali's idea it should be mentioned that some more or less related proposals had been made public earlier. For instance, in an article in the *Frankfurter Allgemeine* in July 1989[4] reference was made to a proposal to establish a kind of European Development Agency to promote small and medium sized enterprises in Central and Eastern Europe. And France's ex-President Valéry Giscard d'Estaing had proposed that the European Community set up a Euro-Polish investment bank to make long-term, low-interest loans to Polish enterprises on the scale of a billion dollars a year.[5] Equally significant was the proposal launched by Mr. A. Herrhausen, the late President of the largest German commercial bank, the Deutsche Bank. He suggested establishing an institution for the modernisation of the economy of Poland, to encourage private initiatives.[6] So, although Mr. Attali apparently scored the goal, the pass had been superb.

Agricultural reform and market-oriented improvement of the infrastructure are, as has been described in chapter 2, key economic reform requirements in a transition process from a centrally planned economy to a market-oriented economy. Therefore, Western assistance for Central and Eastern Europe includes support for these sectors, for which bilateral and existing multilateral channels were used. Before turning to the issue of whether a new, additional multilateral channel is needed, and to the French motives for proposing such a new institution, it is worth looking at the phenomena of international institutions in general and to the European Investment Bank, mentioned by President Mitterrand, in particular.

International institutions

What is an international organisation or institution? It has been argued that although there is no universally accepted definition a minimum requirement for such an organisation might be for its membership, its finance and its field of operation to involve three or more countries.[7] There are many ways of categorising international organisations. One way is to make a distinction between governmental, non-governmental and business organisations. International governmental organisations (IGOs) are generally considered to be those organisations established by treaty. A treaty can be defined as an agreement which establishes binding obligations between the parties, usually though not exclusively, states, and whose terms and provisions are governed by international law.[8] Consequently, IGOs are permanent networks, set up voluntarily, linking states by binding obligations. President Mitterrand proposed to set up a Bank for Europe like the European Investment Bank, which was established by a protocol to the 1957 Treaty of Rome. Therefore he envisaged the creation of a new international governmental organisation.

IGOs can be grouped in several ways; those with specific or more general purposes and those with universal or limited membership. Furthermore international governmental organisations may be predominantly a forum for discussion and future negotiation or service organisations with concrete rules for activities to be carried out.

There are at present some 400 IGOs. The contemporary network of international governmental organisations emerged in the early years of the 19th century. The dominant impulse for the creation of IGOs was a desire to maintain peace in Europe.[9] Factors such as the industrial revolution, which changed the production and trade structure, and the French revolution, which changed the state-society relationship, contributed to the setting up of international organisations. World War I gave a boost to the establishment of organisations to control state violence and to settle disputes between states. More recently welfare considerations played an increasingly important role in the expansion of the IGO networks as governments paid more attention to national welfare. When the time came to re-establish an international economic order after the Second World War most governments were willing to give economic/financial

IGOs a larger role, believing that the amelioration of security problems was at least partially dependent upon progress in the economic and social spheres.[10]

The rules for the post Second World War financial/economic environment were established at the 1944 Bretton Woods conference. In this rule-making conference the victor countries, including the Soviet Union, Poland and Czechoslovakia participated. The United States and to a lesser extent the United Kingdom, represented by Mr. White and Mr. Keynes respectively, dominated the proceedings.[11] In order to impose the idea of a liberal economic order and to prevent the interwar competitive currency depreciations and restrictive trade policies, rules of the game and international financial institutions were set up; the International Monetary Fund, the International Bank for Reconstruction and Development (World Bank) and the International Trade Organisation. The latter institution never came into being and was replaced in 1947 by the General Agreement on Tariffs and Trade.[12]

The major significance of the Bretton Woods institutions was the victorious blow they dealt to the isolationism of the pre-war period.[13] However, this victory over isolationism did not prove to be global as the Soviet Union did not become a member of the IMF and in the following years pressed Poland and Czechoslovakia to terminate their IMF/WB membership, and thus to terminate their participation in the infrastructure of the Western Alliance.[14] Although to some extent the IMF covenant does take into account aspects of a non-market economy the nature of the economy of the Soviet Union was not consistent with the overall philosophy of the established rules of the game. Furthermore the emergence of the Cold War gave the Soviet Union no incentive to join an international system mainly based on the Western economic ideas and it has been argued that Soviet Union membership would have been challenged by the US Congress anyway.[15] The countries of Central and Eastern Europe therefore established their own trade and monetary regional system apart from what became known as the international system based on the Bretton Woods agreements. They established the Council for Mutual Economic Assistance (CMEA or Comecon) in 1949.

The isolationist approach, however, was not maintained fully. As imposing a major change on the Western based international system did not seem likely (as the Third World countries experienced with their unsuccessful demand for a New International Economic Order in the 1970s), a shift towards the Western institutions was the only option left for increased integration in the world economy. In 1972 Romania joined the IMF and the WB, followed by Hungary in 1982 and Poland in 1987. These Central and Eastern European countries were recently accompanied by Bulgaria and Czechoslovakia. Although stressing that the Bretton Woods system is far from perfect (periods of high inflation, large-scale speculative capital flows and capital flight, unemployment, debt crises), the Soviet Union now also considers full participation as a logical step towards establishment of an integrated and universal international trade and monetary system.[16] The same applies to the GATT to which all Central and Eastern European countries, except Albania and the Soviet Union, have become contracting parties: Poland since 1967, Romania since 1971, Hungary since 1973. The Soviet Union was admitted with observer status in May 1990, after a waiting period of four years.[17]

Apart from the universal IGOs already mentioned there are regional economic organisations, such as regional development/investment banks. The late 1950s and the 1960s saw the formation of a number of regional development banks, IGOs which attempt to mobilise capital both within and outside the regions to promote more rapid development of less developed areas. The European Investment Bank was created as part of the European Economic Community. Other regional development banks are the Inter-American Development Bank, the Asian Development Bank, the African Development Bank, the Caribbean Development Bank, the Andean Development Bank etc. In 1971 the CMEA created the International Investment Bank to make loans in order to stimulate growth in the less developed regions of the member countries.[18] In the above given classification regional development banks are specific purpose service organisations with limited membership. The purpose and functions of the European Investment Bank, the institution to which the French President referred in the context of his appeal to set up a new institution to help Central and Eastern Europe, will be looked into in the next section.

The European Investment Bank.[19]

The European Investment Bank, set up in 1958, is an autonomous institution within the European Community structure. The statute of the EIB is a protocol to the 1957 Treaty of Rome, the treaty establishing the European Economic Community. The role of the EIB is to finance capital investment projects within the European Community which contribute towards the balanced regional development of the Community, co-operating closely with the Community's Structural Fund, which provides grants. Those areas whose development is lagging behind or those with declining traditional industries are therefore especially eligible for EIB finance. EIB loans may be granted to public or private sector borrowers throughout the productive sectors embracing infrastructure, energy, industry, services and agriculture.

The EIB, owned by the members states of the European Community, who all subscribed to its capital, operates as a bank, albeit on a non-profit-making basis. Apart from the paid-in capital it raises the bulk of its financial resources on capital markets. It is not funded from the European Community Budget. The six founding members subscribed a starting capital in 1958 of ECU 1 billion. As a result of the enlargement of the European Community from 6 to 12 members and six successive capital increases, the latest a doubling effective from 1 January 1991, the total subscribed capital of the EIB now stands at ECU 57.6 billion (US $67 billion). This makes the EIB next to the World Bank (capital US $171 billion) the largest investment/development bank in the world.

With effect from the latest capital increase the paid-in capital amounts to ECU 4.3 billion, representing 7.5% of the subscribed capital (or 5.4% not counting the free reserves transformed into paid-in capital). The unpaid portion acts as guarantee capital which could be called in to the extent required to meet the obligations towards lenders in respect of its borrowings. Apart from the paid-in capital and reserves the EIB liabilities consist of borrowed resources. At the end of 1989 the outstanding borrowings totalled ECU 43.3 billion, mainly raised by means of medium and long term fixed or variable-rate public loan issues. The EIB has consistently been awarded 'AAA' credit rating, indicating its solid first class borrower reputation. The EIB on-lends the proceeds obtained on the keenest terms and conditions available at the time at cost plus 0.15% to cover administrative expenses. Loans are granted mostly at fixed rates, although they may also carry variable rates or fixed rates revisable after a specific period of generally 5 to 10 years.

The EIB's statute sets the ceiling for outstanding loans and guarantees at 250% of the subscribed capital, at present equalling ECU 144 billion. The total outstanding loans and investments at the end of 1989 amounted to ECU 53.6 billion, giving the EIB sufficient room for continued lending and investment for quite a number of years.

The public and private sector in the countries involved have access to EIB finance on equal terms. The EIB is a complementary source of funds and, within the framework of an appropriate financing plan, can provide loans which will not exceed 50% of the cost of a project. The EIB grants medium and long-term loans, the duration depending on the nature of the project and the life of the assets financed. In general, the terms of the loans can be for up to 10 or 12 years for industrial projects and 12 to 15 years for infrastructure, including energy. Generally loans are made with fixed interest, the rate(s) charged are those in force at the time of contract signature or disbursement. Repayment is made in the currencies disbursed. The EIB requires appropriate security for its loans, usually the guarantee of the state in which the project is located or the guarantee of a first class bank.

In the years 1988–1989 the EIB lent ECU 21.1 billion within the European Community. The main beneficiaries were Italy, which obtained 33.6%, France 13.6%, the United Kingdom 13.4% and Spain 12.1% of the total amount mentioned. Almost half of the lending is for regional development purposes. The remainder for energy resources, infrastructure, protection of the environment and for enhancing the competitive capacity of the Community's industrial sector in the international marketplace and encouraging its integration at European level.

In the years 1988–1989 the EIB lent ECU 1.3 billion outside the European Community in the context of the European Community's development co-operation policy. Under Financial Protocols attached to EC co-operation agreements the EIB finances projects in 12 countries in the Mediterranean region (among others a programme promoting environmental protection in the Mediterranean in co-operation with the World Bank and UNDP) and under the Lomé Conventions in 69 African, Caribbean and Pacific countries (ACP) and Overseas Countries and Territories (OCT).

In 1989 the EIB's Board of Governors, which consists of 12 ministers designated by the member states, authorised lending up to ECU 1 billion for capital investment projects in Poland and Hungary with the guarantee of the Community budget over a period of three years. This decision was taken following an invitation by the Council of the European Communities to the EIB to participate within the framework of a Community programme to help these countries in their progress towards market-oriented economies. The Governors' decision is based on article 18 of the EIB's statute under which the Governors can authorise the EIB to grant loans for investment projects to be carried out outside the member states.

3.2 Possible alternatives

French officials put the proposal to establish a 'Bank for Europe' to implement large-scale priority projects in Central and Eastern Europe on the agenda of the European Community's meeting on current developments in Eastern Europe held in November 1989. In that meeting, a number of the Community members, in particular the Netherlands, West Germany, Italy and Britain,[20] expressed their reservations regarding the necessity of establishing a new international institution. Prime Minister Thatcher, after the meeting, described the bank proposed by France as 'something for the longer term'.[21] France nevertheless pushed its initiative further and put the proposal to establish a new bank, now called Development and Modernization Bank for Eastern Europe,[22] on the agenda of the European (Community) Council, scheduled to meet in Strasbourg on 8 and 9 December 1989. But before turning to the French motives for its initiative and the results of the mentioned Council meeting it is worthwhile investigating whether the functions envisaged for this new bank could be performed by existing international financial institutions.

What functions were envisaged for the new bank? According to the working paper which had been circulated the global purpose of the new bank should be to invest and promote investment in Central and Eastern Europe in order to up-date and expand the productive sectors of the economy of the countries involved. The working paper was based on the charters of the International Finance Corporation and the Asian Development Bank, the latter being the last of the three main regional development banks established and thus the one with the most up-to-date mandate.

Could the objectives mentioned not be achieved by channelling additional funds through existing financial institutions? One option could be to revive in one way or another existing Central and Eastern European institutions, such as the International Investment Bank, an organisation established by 7 CMEA countries in 1971. The fundamental task of the IIB is to grant long term and medium term credits primarily for carrying out projects connected with the international socialist division of labour, specialization and co-operation of production, expenditures for expansion of raw materials and fuel resources for the members' collective interest, and the construction of enterprises of mutual concern to member countries in other branches of the economy, as well as the construction of projects for the development of the national economies of the countries.[23] Using the IIB as a vehicle for Western assistance in reforming Central and Eastern European countries would imply a radical change in its mandate and an extension of its membership beyond the CMEA countries.

Extending an existing regional development/investment bank beyond its original regional membership has been done before. The African Development Bank, created in 1964, initially excluded non-African states from membership. But then, because of the limited resources the bank itself was able to generate, wealthy countries were brought into the institution in 1974 by establishing an affiliate, the African Development Fund.[24] The voting power in the African Development Fund is equally divided between the African Development Bank and the non regional members. But in its day-to-day operations the African Development Fund is controlled by the African Development Bank, which is controlled by the African states.[25] Such a voting structure for the International Investment Bank would, however, be incompatible with the Western policy line regarding support for Central and Eastern Europe as described in section 2.3, being only conditional assistance. Furthermore the IIB membership of countries like Vietnam does not comply with the envisaged European character. Channelling Western support through an existing Eastern European institution, adjusted or not, apparently never appealed to Western governments. But what about the appropriateness of existing development/investment banks, like the (global) International Finance Corporation and the (West) European Investment Bank?

The International Finance Corporation[26]

The International Finance Corporation (IFC), established in 1956, is an affiliate of the World Bank. The proposal for the creation of an institution to encourage foreign investment by private concerns in less developed countries was made by the United Nations Economic and Social Council in 1952, when the World Bank was asked to consult with member governments on the advisability of such action. The role of the World Bank itself is only supplementary to private flows of investments. It does not invest in equity capital and in case of a loan to a private enterprise the charter of the World Bank requires a repayment guarantee by the government of the member country concerned, which limits the Bank's range of action in this respect.

The purpose of the IFC is to further economic development by encouraging the growth of productive private enterprise in member countries—particularly in the less developed countries—thus supplementing the activities of the World Bank. In carrying out this purpose the IFC (a) in association with private investors, assists in financing the establishment, improvement and expansion of productive private enterprises by making investments, without guarantee of repayment by the member government concerned, in cases where sufficient private capital is not available on reasonable terms; (b) seeks to bring together investment opportunities, domestic and foreign private capital, and experienced management and (c) seeks to stimulate and to help create conducive to, the flow of private capital, domestic and foreign, into productive investment in member countries. Occasionally the IFC lends to public enterprises as well where the funds will ultimately be channelled to the private sector. The IFC also provides technical assistance and advisory services to both governments and private companies. To a large extent these functions are similar to those of any investment bank.

Membership of the Corporation is open to all members of the World Bank. In 1989 133 out of the 151 members of the World Bank had joined the IFC. Each member country appoints a Governor. For the IFC members the World Bank Governor is ex officio Governor of the IFC. All the powers of the IFC are vested in the Board of Governors, which may delegate to the Board of Directors most of its powers. The Board of Governors holds an annual meeting in conjunction with that of the Board of Governors of the World Bank. The resident Board of Directors is responsible for the conduct of the general operations of the IFC and is composed ex officio of World Bank Directors. The President of the World Bank (who is by custom a US national) is ex officio chairman of the IFC Board of Directors. The Board of Directors is composed of 22 Directors, who hold office for two years. Each member has 250 votes plus one additional vote for each share of stock held. The United States holds 23.8% of the shares and 22.9% of the voting power, followed by West Germany with 6.7–6.5%, France 6.0–5.8% and Japan 5.2–5.0%.

The initial authorised capital stock of the IFC was US $100 million. Subscriptions have to be paid in dollars or freely convertible currencies. As a result of three successive increases, the latest in December 1985, the total subscribed capital now stands at US $1.3 billion. According to its charter the total subscribed capital (fully paid-in), reserves and surpluses should amount to at least 25% of the total amount of outstanding loans, equity investment and guarantees; hence a gearing ration of 4. In order to maintain its 'AAA' status in the capital market a gearing ration of 2.5 is adhered to. This implies a scope of operations of approximately US $3.3 billion. At the end of 1988 the total outstanding loans, investment and guarantees, the disbursed portfolio, amounted to US $2.3 billion. The share of equity investment totalled US $415 million, being 18.1% of the disbursed portfolio.

IFC loans are generally for 7 to 12 years with a three year period of grace and are made at either fixed or variable rates, while syndicated portions of IFC lending are normally made at floating rates. A commitment fee of 1% is payable on the undisbursed portion of any loan. The IFC neither requires nor accepts government guarantees of repayment on its investments. IFC investments for its own account are generally no more than 25% of the project cost. Over the years the IFC has invested in more than 70 countries, among others, in Yugoslavia. The total investments and loans made available for this country totals more than US $500 million. The bulk of the IFC resources are invested in or lent to middle income developing countries, particularly in Latin-America (notably in Brazil and Mexico).

During 1989–1990, Central and Eastern Europe emerged as an important area requiring increasing emphasis by the IFC in support of the reforms being undertaken there. In Hungary and Poland, the IFC is providing advice on a variety of subjects to governments agencies involved in the process of economic and financial reform and is engaged in a programme of investments, mainly joint ventures, in those countries. The IFC has also assured Bulgaria, Czechoslovakia and Romania of its readiness to assist them. Within the Corporation a new department of investment (Europe) was created for Eastern, Central and Southern Europe.

The European Investment Bank

While the EIB's activities are mainly concentrated within the European Community, its role as an instrument of the Community's co-operation policy with other countries has been widened. In July 1989 the EIB's Board of Governors authorised lending up to ECU 1 billion for capital investment projects in Poland and Hungary with the guarantee of the Community budget over a period of three years. The first projects for Poland and Hungary were approved in June 1990. The first phase of a programme to modernise the Polish State Railway is being supported with ECU 20 million. And an ECU 15 million loan has been advanced to the Hungarian Electric Works Trust. In both countries the EIB gives particular priority to infrastructure projects, the environment and industrial projects, especially those involving joint ventures with European Community enterprises.[27]

The EIB favoured extension of its mandate to other countries of Central and Eastern Europe. Presenting the 1989 annual report to the Governors EIB President, Mr. Ernst-Günther Bröder, stated: 'Other countries in the region may also become eligible for EIB lending in due course, if you agree. The EIB will be pleased to respond favourably to these initiatives, if and when they receive your endorsement'.[28]

In July 1990 the G–24 extended the assistance programme to the German Democratic Republic, Czechoslovakia, Bulgaria and Yugoslavia. Romania, Albania and the Soviet Union did not yet meet the requirements to be eligible for assistance, those being the implementation of measures directed at the establishment of a constitutional state, respect for human rights, multiparty democracy, free elections and the transformation towards market-oriented economies.

The EIB has the advantage of its established position as a permanent borrower on the capital markets on the one hand (in 1961, the year of the EIB's maiden issues, it went to the markets for ECU 21.4 million by means of three issues, in 1980 for ECU 2500 million-73 borrowings and in 1989 for ECU 8700 million-98 borrowings) and of its know-how regarding the development of less developed regions in the European Community and the ACP-countries on the other hand. Furthermore it has already started operations in Poland and Hungary. But one should keep in mind that the primary role of the EIB is and will continue to be within the European Community and that its activities in Central and Eastern Europe is only side-business for the EIB. In the beginning some European Community member countries considered the EIB suitable for the envisaged activities in Central and Eastern Europe. Others favoured a more flexible institution with a private sector bias. Full participation of countries of Central and Eastern Europe in the EIB can be achieved upon their membership of the European Community itself, which is not likely to happen in the near future. However, the EIB has been authorised in the past to implement activities in countries associated with the Community before they actually became full members, such as Spain and Portugal.

All in all the EIB could, as its management proposed, extend its operations to one or more other countries in Central and Eastern Europe, in accordance with the extension of the PHARE programme beyond Poland and Hungary. This happened in March 1991 when the Board of Governors decided to authorise the EIB to lend up to ECU 700 million for projects in Czechoslovakia, Bulgaria and Romania. The decision is in the same terms as that concerning Poland and Hungary.

3.3 Underlying motives

In the previous section it has been shown that existing institutions like the IFC and EIB were starting their operations in Central and Eastern Europe and were well capable of extending their respective roles in this region. Except for the Soviet Union and Albania, all the countries in this region are now members of the IMF and World Bank, a prerequisite for IFC membership and hence assistance. Albania requested to join the Bretton Woods institutions in January 1991 and, as has been mentioned before, the Soviet Union also intends to join these institutions. Additionally, the European Community countries could decide to extend the mandate of the EIB beyond Poland and Hungary.

France's Community partners shared the French feelings that the developments in Central and Eastern Europe were promising but potentially dangerous, and that the West had an obligation to help the reforms to be successful (solidarity, security and stability in Europe). Furthermore they shared the view that part of the assistance should be channelled through development/investment institutions, as this would not require large scale funding to be financed out of national budgets. Still this would not necessitate the establishment of a new institution performing the same functions as existing ones. Why then did France push for the creation of a new institution and why did President Mitterrand call it a highly political decision? According to statements made by President Mitterrand and Mr. Attali there were, apart from the mentioned obligation to help the reforms in Central and Eastern European countries, the following motives: securing assistance to the Soviet Union and the gathering of all European states.

The Soviet Union

In his speech, launching the initiative for a 'Bank for Europe', on 25 October 1989, President Mitterrand had stated '. . . the Soviet Union and, in his historic leading role, Mr. Gorbachev, need to be helped'. Mr. Gorbachev had allowed Central and Eastern European countries to follow their own political and economic paths, which made drastic changes possible, changes that occurred in 1989. But the implementation of *glasnost* and *perestroika* in the Soviet Union itself was, compared to the changes in neighbouring countries, rather slow. Western assistance was only made available for those countries moving rapidly towards democracy and market-oriented economies, and hence was not yet offered to the Soviet Union. The Soviet Union and Mr. Gorbachev needed, according to President Mitterrand, to be helped, if not to be rewarded for the liberal policy towards the other countries in the region.

However, the Soviet Union could not yet receive assistance from existing institutions such as the IFC and the EIB. As has been mentioned before, the Soviet Union was not yet a member of the IMF/World Bank group and therefore was not eligible for IFC support. To include the Soviet Union in the Central and Eastern European programme of the EIB would not only place major constraints on the primary role of the EIB within the European Community, but would also conflict with the conditions set by the European Community for its assistance and, therefore, the EIB's assistance to Central and Eastern Europe. France's 'Bank for Europe' initiative can be regarded as an attempt to create a means to assist Central and Eastern Europe and at the same time to include the Soviet Union: that is, an institution with the broad mandate of assisting the public and private sector in all those Central and Eastern European countries wishing to join.

Common house for Europe

Apart from being a means of including the Soviet Union in Western assistance to Central and Eastern Europe the proposed new institution was supposed to have a global strategic character as well, according to Mr. Attali in a number of press interviews. To quote just one, Darell Delamaide in *Euromoney*:[29] 'The EBRD is a precursor of a necessary higher stage of international organisations and a key part of integration within the Europe-Soviet Union economic block, the first of several new institutions that will form the structure of the "common house for Europe". The EBRD can play the role in the construction of the common house that the European Coal and Steel Community played not long ago in the beginning of building up the European Community. Mediation is crucial, Attali contends, because, the two world wars both resulted from differences in economic development between eastern and western parts of Europe. One of the EBRD's main goals will be to reduce that difference'.

In the same article Mr. Attali's strategic vision of the world economy in the 1990s, as expressed in the recent book *Lignes d'horizon*, is recalled. He foresees the development of two major economic blocs at the heart of the global economy, Japan-United States and Europe-Soviet Union, which will become more and more internally integrated and greater and greater rivals.[30] This coincides with the appeal made by France's President Mitterrand for European Community assistance to Central and Eastern Europe including the Soviet Union. In this context it is interesting to recall that on the one hand the web of IGO networks has greatest density in Western Europe, where the state system was first established and that France holds the highest number of IGO memberships. And that on the other hand the countries in Central and Eastern Europe belong to significantly fewer IGOs than countries of comparable size and level of economic development.[31]

Nevertheless, the question arises of how a new investment bank type IGO, albeit with membership across the whole of Europe and possibly beyond, could become a fore-runner for a 'common house for Europe'? First, this term is usually used in a security context.[32] It is therefore more convincing to consider the ongoing institutional conferences on (European) security to be front-runners for European unity, than a new investment bank. But security issues and economic matters are related to each other. The mutual establishment of a new international financial institution might be a step towards closer economic and political co-operation between Europe and the Soviet Union. However, Mr. Attali's prediction that the new investment bank can play a role in this integration process comparable to the role the ECSC played with regard to the establishment of the European Economic Community is arguable.

At the time of the establishment of the ECSC (1950), France offered partnership with the 'hereditary enemy', Germany, by proposing that both countries should give up national sovereignty in matters that by any reasonable definition could be called 'vital interests'. The coal–steel pool would, according to France's Minister of Foreign Affairs at that time, Mr. Schuman, provide a common basis for economic development, 'the first step in the federation of Europe . . .'.[33] Jean Monnet, who held similar ideas on Europe, added that in order to avoid future wars Germany had to be recognised as having equality of rights.[34] The sharing of vital interests on the basis of equal rights paved the way for the establishment of the European Economic Community in 1957. The concept of the new financial institution as envisaged differs from the ECSC concept, making it difficult if not impossible for the new institution to play a role in the construction of the common house for Europe comparable to the role played by the ECSC in the building up of the European Economic Community.

There are two striking differences. First, the extent to which the international institution involved can act independently from its member states as an international actor.[35] The degree of autonomous decision–making power is a key element influencing the opportunity for an international institution to become an important actor in international relations. There are only few international institutions in which the decision-makers do not act as representatives of member states but in their individual capacities, responsible to the institution alone. The ECSC is such a supranational institution, whereas the envisaged new institution will not have a supranational character. The ultimate responsible body in the latter institution will not be an independent 'High Authority' but, similar to the EIB and ADB structure, a Board of Governors composed of high ranking national government officials.

Secondly, the function of making foreign funds available on commercial terms, albeit at the best rates available, does not match the ECSC's function of sharing vital interests on equal terms. None the less, France's policy vis-a-vis Germany, which at the time resulted in the establishment of the ECSC, could have played a role in the French 'Bank for Europe' initiative as well. This issue will be dealt with in the next section.

But before turning to this issue, it should be mentioned that the establishment of a new international financial institution such as a development/investment bank, which the Central and Eastern European countries could help design and in which they can participate from the start, can be considered as a kind of goodwill signal emphasising the mutual benefits of integrating the Eastern economies in the global system. As it was accurately put: 'The general feeling seems to be that if existing institutions could perform the functions of the new institution, the creation of a new multilateral organisation with participation of both East and West sets an important precedent for co-operation'.[36]

The embedding of Germany

In his speech on 25 October 1989 before the European Parliament, launching the 'Bank for Europe' initiative, the French President touched on the German issue in the following way: 'Who among us has not heard groups of intellectuals, journalists, politicians in debate? Eastern Europe is breaking up, but also opening up. Could this be the prelude to a far-reaching transformation, to the collapse and dislocation of Western Europe? And of course, such discussions always revolve around the two Germanies'.[37] Indeed, as David S. Yost wrote in an article in *Foreign Affairs*,[38] the remarkable developments in Central and Eastern Europe in 1989 have upset long-standing assumptions of French security policy.

Yost argues along the following lines. Since the 1960s French security policy has been based upon among others a West Germany anchored in NATO, dependent on allied security commitments and particularly interested in obtaining French cooperation regarding West European economic integration and within and outside other multilateral political, economic and military institutions. Now, given the events in Central and Eastern Europe, Western Europe has to organise its security relations on a radically new basis. Paris agrees with other Western governments that movements in the Soviet Union towards democratisation, economic liberalisation and a peaceful settlement of the nationalities issues should be encouraged. France joined West Germany in urging their Western partners to provide immediate economic aid to the Soviet Union. But the French government's motives in this regard appear to include considerations beyond simple economic and political reform in the Soviet Union. Above all, France is profoundly interested in having a common policy with Germany and, somewhat paradoxically, in competing with the Germans for privileged relations with Moscow. According to Yost, France's determination to compete for influence in the Soviet Union and Eastern Europe reflects one of the many French preoccupations and anxieties regarding Germany in the new Europe.

In political and economic contacts with the Soviet Union and Eastern Europe West Germany had clearly taken the lead. West Germany's Ostpolitik, or Eastern policy, initiated in 1966, aimed at improving political and diplomatic contacts between the Federal Republic and the East, especially East Germany by means of trade liberalisation, participation in joint ventures with East European governments, credits, and technology transfers. As a leading trading partner of the Soviet Union and Eastern Europe and in continuing pursuit of its Ostpolitik, West Germany took a strong interest in increasing economic relations with the East and responded positively to their interest in increased political ties with the European Community and German firms, with the support of their government, aggressively pursued trade and joint venture opportunities.[39] Its share in the Soviet trade turnover with Western countries amounted to 18% in the late 1980s, whereas the French share dropped from 10% in 1985 to 7% in 1989.[40]

Before 1989 the French had implicitly assumed, like almost everyone else, that German unification would remain a remote possibility, due to seemingly permanent Soviet policy imperatives. But Mr. Gorbachev embarked on a different course. He accepted not only the establishment of non-communist regimes in Central and Eastern Europe, including East Germany, but also German unification. Hannes Adomeit reveals in an article in *Problems of Communism* that even though Gorbachev, in 1988 and 1989, did not actively promote the unification of Germany, he did in all probability consider it a possible and, for the Soviet Union, an acceptable consequence of his policy conceptions. Once unity of Germany appeared on the European political agenda, he quickly adjusted to the idea and was willing to deal with it in a constructive way.[41]

As it became evident that the assumption that German unification would remain a remote possibility was mistaken, French politicians and analysts began to recognise that the postwar political and security arrangements, by postponing any resolution of the German question, had elevated France's status and influence in Europe. The likely consequence of German unity and Soviet retreat could then include an economically superpowerful Germany, politically dominant in Central Europe and a France reduced to a secondary role. France called attention to the democratic history of the Federal Republic of Germany and its commitment to NATO and the EC.[42] In his speech to the European Parliament President Mitterrand drew the conclusion that the destruction of the system or structures of the East should lead to the strengthening and acceleration of the political construction of Europe.[43]

In several press articles the relation between the heavy political pressure France used to establish a new, basically European, institution to assist the Central and Eastern European countries in their transition process and the German economic and assistance policy towards the East has been pointed out. The *Frankfurter Allgemeine* published an article stating that the French by means of an Eastern Europe bank were aiming at influencing the German assistance.[44] And the British Overseas Development

Institute in its briefing paper on the EBRD referred to this issue in the following way: 'The French probably had their own reasons for proposing the bank, not the least to provide some counter-balance to the prospect of a Europe dominated by German economic might'.[45]

Taking into account the positive political and economic results of West Germany's Ostpolitik and the unclear situation regarding the possibility and timing of Germany's re-unification in the second half of 1989, as well as the French reluctance at the time to accept the momentum of the unification process, and furthermore the original Soviet condition that a united Germany should not be member of the Western security alliance NATO, there is a good deal of evidence that the embedding of Germany could have been another reason for France launching its political EBRD initiative in those uncertain months in the second half of 1989.

French *gloire*

And last, but not least, French *gloire* might have played a role. France's foreign policy is well known for its initiatives, within or without the consensus context of the European Community, and France can be said to have developed a taste for theatrical diplomatic gestures. These are qualities that most of France's partners in the European Community have not developed to the same extent, or at least do not display to the same extent. These characteristics of French foreign policy in combination with the rapid political and economic developments in Central and Eastern Europe in the course of 1989 and the mere fact that France held the six-months rotating presidency in the European Community in the second half of 1989 might have inspired France to launch yet another of its rather bold political initiatives. And by doing so it could only gain. In the case of the European Community not endorsing the initiative, France had at least showed its goodwill towards Central and Eastern European countries in general, and towards the Soviet Union in particular. On the other hand, if the political pressure to adopt the initiative proved successful, France would not only get the credit for being the initiator of the project with great political visibility, but also be in an excellent position to influence the forthcoming negotiations.

3.4 Endorsement by EC-partners

France had taken stock of the reactions of its European Community partners regarding its proposal to establish a 'Bank for Europe' to develop and modernize the productive sector in Central and Eastern Europe in November 1989. As has been outlined in a previous section France's partners recognised the importance of the productive and competitive sector as a key factor in the transformation of centrally planned economies into market-oriented economies. Furthermore they shared France's view that Western assistance for this sector was needed to facilitate the transition process. However, at that time, some of France's partners did not share France's view that it was necessary to establish a new international financial institution. The assistance required could be made available satisfactorily by means of existing bilateral and multilateral channels.

France's partners had neither much time nor room to manoeuvre. President Mitterrand had made the appeal to establish a new investment-type bank public without consulting its Community partners in advance. There is much to say that this was done precisely with this effect in mind. Furthermore, France was pressing for a political decision before the end of 1989, when Ireland would take over the six-months presidency of the Community. There was not much time to investigate possible alternatives.[46] On the other hand, the Community had been given a co-ordinating role by the G–24 countries in the assistance of Central and Eastern Europe. In the period preceding the Council's meeting in December 1989 the developments in the region towards democracy spread rapidly from one country to another. Dramatic changes occurred in the German Democratic Republic and in Romania. This was not the moment to block an initiative, already made public, to extend the assistance to Central and Eastern Europe. The need for more assistance involving more countries of the region became urgent and hence, the announcment of an additional European goodwill signal less odd. France's initiative became a 'political appeal that no European Community government felt able to resist'.[47] And if the proposal were accepted, it would not be difficult for France's Community partners to make a virtue of necessity.

The establishment of a new development/investment bank

for Central and Eastern Europe could result in the following benefits:

(a) a co-ordinating role for the new institution being the only one with a mandate strictly confined to Central and Eastern Europe;

It makes sense to have an institution that can attract strong support from the nearby countries and generate special expertise about the region involved.[48] Being the single international economic/financial institution focusing entirely on Central and Eastern Europe the new institution might acquire the role of policy co-ordination unit and hence contribute to the overall co-ordination of Western assistance and might develop into the key institution monitoring economic reform in Central and Eastern Europe.[49]

(b) Keeping the option open of not having to extend the EIB mandate beyond Poland and Hungary;

The EIB is, in principle, an institution created by the European Community to perform activities within the Community. The extension of its field of operations in Poland and Hungary has been described in a previous section. Extending the scope of the EIB to more countries in Central and Eastern Europe, and in particular to the Soviet Union, as well as involving non EC-OECD countries in EIB context as potential donors could not be realised without major adjustments in the EIB's mandate and structure. Changing a well established Community institution into something as yet unknown was not very attractive. The EIB, on the other hand, could well be involved in the creation of a new, more or less similar institution for a different group of countries. Furthermore this would leave the possibility of extending the EIB mandate in Central and Eastern Europe on a selective basis.

(c) keeping financial assistance to Central and Eastern Europe separated from financial assistance to the Third World;

Proposals for a switch of Western aid from the Third World to Central and Eastern Europe, floated by several sources in the autumn of 1989,[50] provoked sharp reactions in the developing as well as the developed world. A separate bank, obtaining its funds on the international capital markets, would diminish the fear of government funds being diverted from the Third World.

France's hesitant Community partners changed their perception and the proposal was endorsed during the Council meeting in Strasbourg on 8 and 9 December 1989. 'At this time of profound and rapid change the Community is and must remain a point of reference and influence. It remains the cornerstone of a new European architecture and, in its will to openness, the mooring for a future European equilibrium'.[51] According to the meeting record the European Bank for Reconstruction and Development as it was now named 'will be to promote, in consultation with the IMF and World Bank, productive and competitive investment in the states of Central and Eastern Europe, to reduce, where appropriate, any risks related to the financing of their economies, to assist the transition towards a more market-oriented economy and to speed up the necessary structural adjustments. The states of Central and Eastern Europe concerned will be able to participate in the capital and management of this bank, in which the Member States, the Community and the European Investment Bank will have a majority holding. Other countries, and in particular the other member countries of the OECD, will be invited to participate. The European Council hopes that the European Bank for Reconstruction and Development will be set up as soon as possible. The European Council requests that the negotiations are opened in January 1990. The European Investment Bank will play a key role in preparing the way for this new institution'.[52]

Two elements were settled in advance of the forthcoming negotiations. The first one being that the new institution is supposed to operate in consultation with the IMF and World Bank. It should not present an alternative to these institutions. Secondly, a decision about the membership issue was taken. France had been ambiguous in this respect; on the one hand it had wished to keep it European, on the other hand it had mentioned the possibility of inviting others as well. The Community, although stressing the European character of the new Bank, favoured the participation of at least the G–24 countries (OECD countries); hence invited the United States and Japan to join.

The endorsement of the proposal to establish a new institution can and should be labelled as a remarkable French success. France had obtained a favourable decision on the principle.

Chapter Four

The EBRD Negotiations

In December 1989 the European Council endorsed the French initiative to establish a new investment/development bank type of international institution, now called the European Bank for Reconstruction and Development, to help Central and Eastern European countries move from centrally planned economies to market-oriented economies. The Council expressed the hope that the EBRD would be set up as soon as possible and requested the negotiations be opened in January 1990. The momentum was not lost. The first meeting of the intergovern tal conference to determine the statutes of the EBRD, organised by France, was held in Paris on 15 and 16 January1990.[1] The first part of this chapter focuses on the participants in the negotiations and the way the conference was organised.

The constitutive negotiations lasted only four and a half months. The delegations were able to draw on the statutes and the experience of other development/investment banks such as the World Bank, the International Finance Corporation, the European Investment Bank and the Asian Development Bank. Thus, the resulting Agreement contained many of the provisions of these institutions. But there are remarkable differences as well. These unique aspects of the EBRD will be the subject of the second section of this chapter. The third and final section highlights a number of topics that played a major role in the negotiations.

4.1 Participants and procedures

The first constitutive meeting, organised by France, was held in Paris on 15 and 16 January 1990. It is interesting to note that the meeting was held in Paris and not in Dublin, the capital of the country holding the six-months Community presidency in the period concerned, i.e. in the first half of 1990. The same applies to the fact that not an Irish official, but a Frenchman, Mr. Attali, was chairing the meeting. These two points indicated that the operation was (still) regarded by France's Community partners to be more a French than a Community project. From French perspective it might be argued that it was a project beyond Community scope. Anyway, France's leading role was not challenged in this respect.

Launching the initiative President Mitterrand had indicated that the new institution should have on its Board of Directors the 12 European countries, others such as Poland and Hungary and 'why not the Soviet Union, and yet others'.[2] Endorsing the French initiative to establish a new international financial institution to assist Central and Eastern European countries in their transition towards market-oriented economies, the European Council referred to the membership issue in the following way: 'The States of Central and Eastern Europe concerned will be able to participate in the capital and management of this bank, in which the Member States, the Community and the European Investment Bank will have a majority holding. Other countries, and in particular the other member countries of the OECD, will be invited to participate'.[3]

Consequently the first constitutive meeting was attended by the 12 European Community member countries, the European Community, the European Investment Bank, eight Central and Eastern European countries (all except Albania) and the remaining 12 non-EC OECD countries. Two non-OECD countries joined the conference as well, Cyprus and Malta. Both countries are associated to the European Community. Thirty-six countries and institutions participated in the first meeting. Most delegations were headed by high ranking Ministry of Finance officials, as in most countries the Ministry of Finance has primary responsibility for multilateral and regional development/investment banks. A list of the names and functions of the respective delegation leaders is attached in appendix 1.

In his speech welcoming the delegations to the first constitutive session, President Mitterrand repeated that other countries could join as well: 'While the initiative is European, the project goes far further. In fact it is open to all those wishing to take part, I cannot define it more broadly or fully'.[4] And indeed, in the following months the number of potential shareholders increased to 42 as delegations of South Korea, Liechtenstein, Morocco, Israël, Egypt and finally Mexico joined the negotiations.[5]

However, with the notable exception of South Korea which aimed at boosting economic and political ties with the Soviet Union,[6] the appropriateness of the participation of at least some of these newcomers can be questioned. Most of them have a per capita income that does not exceed the average per capita income of the Central and Eastern European recipient countries. And some of these countries have a foreign debt of a magnitude that exceeds the foreign debt of recipient countries like Poland and Hungary. Why should these countries give financial support to (measured in per capita income) richer countries, or, if you like, less poor countries? The Asian Development Bank for instance has a provision in its charter stating that non-regional members should be developed countries.

There is an obvious answer: procurement. Existing development/investment banks give preference to contractors and suppliers of the member countries of the respective institutions. Not surprisingly some of the delegations, notably Japan, Turkey, Cyprus and Malta, favoured similar restriction of the tenders financed by EBRD funds to the member countries. The newcomers might have wished to join the new institution in order to qualify their enterprises to participate in tenders for projects to be financed by the new institution.[7] However, a large majority of the negotiating parties rejected this kind of protectionism and favoured open procurement procedures. Consequently it was decided that 'the Bank shall place no restriction upon the procurement of goods and services from any country from the proceeds of any loan, investment or other financing . . .' (article 13 (xii) of the Agreement). In the Chairman's Report on the Agreement it is explained that the open procurement policy is intended as a gesture to give less developed countries, not members, the opportunity to tender for EBRD contracts[8] on equal terms with Bank members.

The decision to introduce an open procurement procedure

did not lead to any of the newcomers leaving. Not only might this have been rather embarrassing but there remained other benefits as well. First, a shareholder could still expect to be in a better position regarding tenders than non-shareholders, and the institution could be expected to acquire extensive knowledge about the economic developments in Central and Eastern Europe; information not easily obtainable elsewhere for developing countries. And, secondly, political considerations might have played a role.

All participating countries and organisations signed the Agreement establishing the EBRD. The total membership of 42 is fairly in line with the membership of the three main regional development banks, the Inter-American, African and Asian Development Bank. But there is striking difference in the sub-totals for recipient and donor countries. In the three previously mentioned regional development banks, contrary to the EBRD, the recipient countries outnumber donor countries.

The first constitutive meeting in January 1990 was followed by two plenary meetings in March and April 1990, between which a group of technical experts was assigned the task of negotiating and amending concept articles and working out compromise proposals. The discussions in the three plenary meetings concerned, in particular, the following issues: the political motivation behind the creation of the EBRD, the purpose and functions of the bank, the total capital stock of the new institution, the division of shares and voting power, the operational approach, in particular the recipient status of the Soviet Union, the use of the European Currency Unit as means of payment and valuation of capital subscriptions, and last, but not least, the issue of the appointment of the first president and the location of the EBRD headquarters. These issues will be dealt with in subsequent sections of this chapter.

4.2 Political and economic orientation

The charters of the World Bank and the three previously mentioned regional development/investment banks are not based on a particular political nor economic orientation. These institutions deal with the government in place and do not confine themselves to any type of government or government policy.

On the contrary, the charters of these institutions specifically prohibit them and their staff from being influenced by political considerations or by the political character of their respective members.[9] Only economic and social development considerations are relevant to their decisions. However, sometimes political considerations do play a role too. For example gross violation of human rights can lead to temporary suspension of lending by existing institutions to particular countries, such as the World Bank's lending to China as a result of the Tiananmen Square violence in the summer of 1989.

On the other hand, political and human rights conditions play an important role in the bilateral development co-operation policy of many countries and in the policies of many non-governmental organisations active in the field of development co-operation. This approach was also adopted by the G-24 countries with regard to their co-ordinated bilateral assistance to Central and Eastern Europe. As described in chapter 2, Western assistance was only made available to those countries in that region moving decisively towards democracy and market-oriented economies. A large majority of the Western group favoured copying the G-24 conditional approach with regard to their co-ordinated bilateral assistance to Central and Eastern Europe in the charter of the new institution. Thus envisaging the creation of a development/investment bank with a political and economic orientation. An orientation that would not only refer to the commitment to political and economic reform but also to actual implementation of the reform policies.

The introduction in the bank's charter of provisions stipulating that recipient countries should be committed to the fundamental principles of multiparty democracy, respect for human rights as well as to market economics was a rather difficult issue to solve. In the constitutive conference the delegations of the Central and Eastern European countries, in particular the Soviet Union's, finally accepted the linkage between eligibility and commitment. Obviously their governments were (at least at the time of the conference) serious about their commitment to democracy and market economics.[10]

Commitment to democracy and market economics is one thing, but what about putting this commitment into practice? Should the conditionality of the new bank be extended to include the application of this commitment as well? In this respect opinions, not surprisingly, differed. Such an extension of the bank's conditions obviously did not fit into the original French concept. Some of France's Community partners supported the more lenient French line, but others favoured including in the bank's charter the necessity of actual implementation of the reform policies. Thus there was not Community consensus. This was not an isolated case. The Community meetings that preceded the plenary conference sessions did not prove very successful in reaching common points of view. With regard to the issue of whether to limit access to the bank to recipient countries actually implementing in practice the reform commitments, the United States and Japan took a firm stance. They considered the extended conditionality essential. The US delegation made it clear that the United States would not join the new institution if their view on this issue was not accepted. Without unity in the Community views France could not hold on to its own concept of no political conditions. Consequently in the end the United States, after tough negotiations in particular with the Soviet Union, got its way. Not only would the charter of the bank refer to the reform commitment but also make practical implementation of the reform policies a condition for recipient countries to have access to the funds of the bank.

The political and economic orientation of the bank is outlined in the preamble and, in particular, in the first article of its charter. The Agreement establishing the European bank for Reconstruction and Development starts with the following preamble:

The contracting parties,
Committed to the fundamental principles of multiparty democracy, the rule of law, respect for human rights and market economics;
Recalling the Final Act of the Helsinki Conference on Security and Cooperation in Europe, and in particular its Declaration on Principles;
Welcoming the intent of Central and Eastern European countries to further the practical implementation of multiparty democracy, strengthening democratic institutions, the rule of law and respect for human rights and their willingness to implement reforms in order to evolve towards market-oriented economies;
Considering the importance of close and coordinated cooperation in order to promote the economic progress of Central and Eastern European countries to help their economies become more

internationally competitive and assist them in their reconstruction and development and thus to reduce, where appropriate, any risks related to the financing of their economies;
Convinced that the establishment of a multilateral financial institution which is European in its basic character and broadly international in its membership would help serve these ends and would constitute a new and unique structure of cooperation in Europe;
Have agreed to establish hereby the European Bank for Reconstruction and Development (hereinafter called "the Bank") which shall operate in accordance with the following:

And article 1 of the agreement describes the purpose of the bank:

In contributing to economic progress and reconstruction, the purpose of the Bank shall be to foster the transition towards open market-oriented economies and to promote private and entrepreneurial initiative in the Central and Eastern European countries committed to and applying the principles of multi-party democracy, pluralism and market economics.

As a consequence, the way to measure the implementation of policies directed at the introduction of democracy and market economics became an issue. Under what norms and time-table should progress be monitored, and which human rights should be taken into consideration? This was difficult to put on paper in detail. It was decided not to do this at all by instructing the Board of Directors of the bank to review the performances of the respective recipient countries in this respect. Article 8.3 contains the provision with regard to this review:

In cases where a member might be implementing policies which are inconsistent with Article 1 of this Agreement, or in exceptional circumstances, the Board of Directors shall consider whether access by a member to Bank resources should be suspended or otherwise modified and may make recommendations accordingly to the Board of Governors. Any decision on these matters shall be taken by the Board of Governors by a majority of not less than two-thirds of the Governors, representing not less than three-fourths of the total voting power of the members.

To this article 11.2 adds:

The Board of Directors shall review at least annually the Bank's operations and lending strategy in each recipient country to ensure that the purpose and the functions of the Bank, as set out in Articles 1 and 2 of this Agreement, are fully served. . . . The said review shall involve the consideration of, inter alia, each recipient country's progress made on decentralization, demono-polization and privatization . . .

Although only experience will show to what extent political and market economy considerations will play a decisive role in the operations of the EBRD, it is likely that in the political con-ditions will sooner or later result in tough discussions and diffi-cult decisions. An option for the bank will be to follow the G-24 policy with regard to assistance to Central and Eastern Europe, in particular since the policy in this respect towards the Soviet Union has been dealt with separately during the negotiations.

Recipient status of the Soviet Union

In his speech to the European Parliament, launching the EBRD-initiative, France's President Mitterrand had suggested having representatives from Poland, Hungary and 'why not the Soviet Union, and yet others' (note 11) on the Board of Directors, alongside representatives of the 12 European Community countries. As has been described in chapter 3, involvement of the Soviet Union in the European support-schemes for Central and Eastern Europe was a key French motive for its EBRD initi-ative. Consequently, the Soviet Union had been invited to join the first consitutive meeting of the potential shareholders of the EBRD in January 1990. All Central and East European countries (except Albania) participated in this meeting. However, the issue whether the Soviet Union would be granted recipient status and if so whether this should be limited, became the subject of tough negotiations[12] The US delegation made it clear to the con-ference participants that the US Congress would probably object to full recipient status for the Soviet Union.[13] This policy stance jeopardized the French objective to establish a new international financial institution able to assist all Central and Eastern European countries.

In a way history repeated itself, as, at least to some extent, a parallel can be drawn with the different points of view regarding the Soviet Union's recipient status in the context of the American Marshall Plan funds in 1947. In his memoirs Robert Marjolin,[14] the first Secretary General of the Organisation for European Economic Co-operation, the fore-runner of the OECD, recalled that France and Britain asked the Soviet Union to join them in considering how a European Recovery Pro-gramme financed through Marshall Plan funds might be developed. He continues that the Soviet Union was prepared to accept American aid, of course, but refused it being tied to any condition, such as supervision of the use of funds or an assurance that Eastern Europe would progressively open up to trade with Western Europe. The result was the breakdown of the conference organised by France and Britain and the consequent refusal of the Soviet Union and all the Soviet-dominated countries to participate in the Marshall Plan. Marjolin remarks that the breakdown of the conference was 'greeted with a sigh of relief by many in Europe and in the United States, seeing how difficult, if not impossible, it would have been to get the US Congress to approve aid which would have gone in part to a country and its satellites that each day revealed a little more to be the determined adversaries of everything the West and its free-market system represented'.[14]

In 1989 increasing trade with the West is a policy objective of the Soviet Union and conditions on the use of funds made available on favourable terms is not a taboo anymore. Hence, contrary to 1947, the Soviet Union is interested in financial support from the West, even on conditional terms. Although the EBRD funds are not grants, as was aid under the Marshall Plan, but investments and loans at market rates (albeit at the best rates obtainable) the United States still threatened not to join the new bank if the Soviet Union became from the start a major borrower from the organisation.[15] Japan supported the United States in this tough line, but, most of the West European countries considered Soviet borrowing acceptable, if not, like France, desirable. The United States realised that it could not block Soviet access to the bank completely. Insisting on this point could imply that the bank would go ahead without the participation of the United States,[16] a development not favoured by the United States or the other countries, particularly the United Kingdom.

The negotiations concerning the recipient status of the Soviet Union produced a compromise, formulated in a rather odd way. On the one hand an article was introduced into the Agreement that offered a recipient country the opportunity over a period of three years, beginning after entry into force of the Agreement, to voluntarily limit its access to the bank's resources to the amount of paid-in capital (article 8.4). Such a request should be attached to the Agreement as an integral part of it. And on the other hand the delegation leader of the Soviet Union informed the conference chairman in writing that his government was prepared to limit its access to the bank's resources pursuant to the before mentioned paragraph of the Agreement. It reads '. . . I would like to inform you that my government is prepared to limit its access to the Bank's resources . . . the total amount of any assistance thus provided by the Bank would not exceed the total amount of the cash disbursed and the promissory notes issued by the Soviet Union for its shares'. This letter, attached as a protocol to the Agreement, is reproduced in full in appendix 3. It goes without saying that this provision in the EBRD charter is unique.

Anticipating the next section on finance this compromise regarding the recipient status of the Soviet Union implied the following. Given the capital subscription of the Soviet Union of ECU 600 million and the 30%–70% division between paid-in and callable capital[17] its access to EBRD funds, amounts to ECU 180 million.

Obviously France had not succeeded in achieving full recipient status for the Soviet Union, which had been one of the aims in its EBRD initiative. France had reasons to be flexible, as described in chapter 2, and restricted recipient status was better than the non-participation of the Soviet Union. Furthermore the position of the conference chairman might have played a role. As a delegation leader of a smaller European Community country remarked 'from the moment when Attali was a candidate to the presidency, he did what had to be done to get the support of the US and Japan'.[18]

The Soviet Union in its turn accepted the compromise as well, albeit reluctantly. In the above-mentioned letter the Soviet Union expressed its intention to become an equal member of the bank and linked its preparedness to limit its access to the bank's resources to fears of a number of countries that due to the size of its economy the Soviet Union may become the principal recipient of credits of the bank. This was a face-saving linkage, given the operating principle that the bank shall not allow a disproportionate amount of its resources to be used for the benefit of any member (article 13 iv). In an article in *European Affairs* the Soviet delegation leader later explained that the Soviet

Union, not gaining any commercial benefit from participation in the EBRD during the first three years of its operations, treats its opportunities to obtain loans from the EBRD as first steps towards diversification of its foreign borrowing, towards participation in international tenders, and towards access to the Bank's technical assistance.[19]

At the end of the three year period the decision to allow access beyond the paid-in capital has to be taken by a majority of not less than three-quarters of the Board of Governors of the bank, representing not less than 85% of the total voting power of the members (article 8.4 (iii)). This gives the US together with one other major shareholder, e.g. Japan (combined voting power 18.5%), joint veto power. In this respect the EBRD negotiations, although not intentionally, supported Mr. Attali's view of the development of two major blocks at the heart of the global economy, United States–Japan and Europe–Soviet Union.[20]

4.3 Particular topics

Capital stock, division of shares and voting power

The function of an institution like the EBRD is to borrow funds on capital markets on the best terms available and on-lend these resources to the recipient countries, as these countries are not in a position to obtain those favourable borrowing conditions themselves or to acquire funds in the international capital markets at all. In order to be able to borrow funds on capital markets the institution needs, just as commercial banks and enterprises, funds of its own, that is to say capital subscribed by its owners, the shareholders. The capital provided by the shareholders acts as guarantee capital to meet the obligations towards its lenders. The size of the capital provided by the shareholders therefore to a large extent determines the borrowing capacity of the institution or organisation involved.

France suggested a starting capital for the EBRD of ECU 15 billion, equivalent to US $17.6 billion (ECU–dollar rate December 1989). The United States, Japan and Britain considered ECU 5 billion to be appropriate.[21] Taking into account that these countries would be among the largest shareholders budgetary reasons might have led them to be more modest in this respect than France, the initiator of the project. In the end the delegations agreed to a starting capital of ECU 10 billion, equivalent to

US $11.7 billion (ECU–dollar rate December 1989). The authorized capital is divided into one million shares having a par value of ECU 10,000 each.

Compared to the actual authorised capital of the World Bank (over US $170 billion) this is a rather modest amount. The (initial) capital basis of the EBRD is also smaller than those of the other three main regional development banks (the Inter-American, African and Asian Development Bank). However, taking into account that in the case of these regional development banks recipient countries greatly outnumber the recipient countries in the EBRD, then on average, far more funds can be made available by the EBRD to each recipient country.

The subscribed capital can be paid-in fully or be paid-in only partially. The unpaid portion acts as guarantee capital which can be called in. For the two largest development/investment banks, the World Bank[22] and the European Investment Bank[23] the paid-in part of the total capital is 7.5%. For the other three regional development banks the paid-in ratio varies from 7.6 to 25%. The capital of the International Finance Corporation, the World Bank affiliate supplying funds to the private sector without the necessity of state guarantee, is paid-in fully, i.e. a ration of 100%. For the EBRD, lending to the private sector and the public sector, the paid-in ratio of the subscribed capital was set at 30%.[24] Given the lending objectives on the one hand and the ceiling for outstanding loans and investments on the other hand (100% of the subscribed capital for the EBRD,[25] World Bank and EIB 250%) the EBRD paid-in capital ratio can be considered to be in line with the existing practice.

From the start, France and the other European Community members aimed at a combined share majority for the European Community group in order to stress the basic European character of the new institution. Among themselves they settled for a distribution similar to the share division in the European Investment Bank.[26] As far as the shares of the recipient countries were concerned the starting point was their share division in the IIB. A major issue in the negotiations was the share to be allocated to the Soviet Union, if any at all. The US would have preferred to restrict the participation of the Soviet Union to that of an observer.[27] This was not acceptable to other delegations. A proposal was floated to give all the major countries, France, Britain, Italy, Germany, the United States, Japan and the Soviet Union an equal share of 8.5%. This was not what the United States had in mind and its delegation managed to increase the US share to 10%; the Soviet Union's share dropped to 6%. At the end of the day the following distribution of the shares was reached: 12 European Community countries 45% (four largest countries each 8.5175%), European Community and EIB each 3%, the US 10%, Japan 8.5175% and the recipient countries in total 13.45%. The share division is reproduced in full in appendix 2. The European Community members and institutions total share in the capital (and votes) amounts 51%. This majority can not be reduced by means of future capital increases or extension of the number of shareholders (article 5.2).

The unification of Germany on 3 October 1990 made it necessary to reshuffle the original agreed share division. In the course of October 1990 the German Finance Minister, Mr. Theo Waigel, informed the EBRD President-designate by letter that Germany did not intend to take up the share of the capital stock subscribed by the former German Democratic Republic.[28] Germany apparently preferred to keep its share in line with the other three large European Community members. It was decided to reserve the share allocated to the German Democratic Republic, 1.55%, for potential new members. The Agreement does not offer a country the possibility receiving 'recipient' status for part of its territory. It is understood that Germany will not request such an amendment nor oppose it if tabled. This implies that instead of the EBRD it is now the EIB that will support the eastern region of Germany, as it clearly qualifies as a less privileged region of the European Community.

The payment of the paid-in part of the subscription is to be made in five equal instalments of 20%. The first instalment is due within 60 days from the date of the Agreement coming into force, and the remaining four instalments become due successively in one year increments.

The relation between shareholding and voting power in the various development/investment banks differs considerably.[29] In the EBRD each shareholder has votes equal to the number of its subscribed shares in the capital stock of the bank.[30] The general rule for the Board of Governors' and the Board of Directors' decisions is that matters are decided by a (qualified) majority of the votes cast. However, various decisions require different majorities:

- day-to-day decisions: Directors, simple majority of the voting power of the members voting,
- matters of general policy: Directors, two-thirds majority of the total voting power of the members voting,
- admitting new members, increase of the authorised capital, suspension or modifying of lending to a country found not to be complying to the conditions of the bank, termination of operations: two-thirds majority of the Governors not representing less than three-quarters of the total voting power of the members and
- changing a member's eligibility to borrow: three-quarters of the Governors representing not less than 85% of the total voting power of the members.

It is important to note that resort to voting is rather uncommon in this kind of institution where most decisions are reached through consensus.[31]

Lending to private–public sector

One of the most difficult issues to resolve during the constitutive meetings turned out to be defining the scope of access of the public sector in Central and Eastern European countries to EBRD resources. Endorsing the initiative in December 1989, the European Council stated that the function of the EBRD 'will be to promote . . . productive and competitive investment in the States of Central and Eastern Europe . . .'.[32] Productive and competitive investment can be conducted by the private sector as well as the public sector. The World Bank and the other three main regional development banks are lending to states and require guarantees of the governments involved. The World Bank's IFC affiliate on the other hand is authorised to lend to the private sector without the obligation to obtain government guarantee.

In his welcoming speech to delegations participating in the first constitutive meeting in Paris on 15 January 1990, President Mitterrand recalled the European Council's decision to create a bank for development and reconstruction, whose task is to promote 'productive and competitive investment in the States of Central and Easter Europe . . .'.[33] However, this concept was not adopted. Among others the delegations of the United States and the United Kingdom opposed funds going to the public sector, arguing that this would amount to subsidising failing socialism.[34]

They insisted on changing the 'productive and competitive' concept to 'private'. This proposal to restrict the operations of the EBRD to the private sector was strongly objected to by the Soviet delegation as the Soviet law on private ownership was, to put it mildly, not in favour of foreign investment and foreign ownership.

Most of the other European countries, although favouring emphasis on the private sector, did not share the view expressed by the United States and Britain either. One of their delegation leaders gave the following explanation in this regard: 'As Europeans, we view American attitudes towards the public sector as dogmatic. They perceive it as necessarily negative. We agree on promoting private enterprise, but we'd like less rigidity. Their attitudes show a lack of trust in the board of administration'.[35] The West German Minister for Economic Affairs put it even more strongly: 'I hope this new institution can make a very valuable contribution to building modern infrastructure so commercial banks can play their proper role in helping companies make the switch from command economies to free markets'.[36]

Concentrating exclusively on the private sector would have severe disadvantages. First, the private sector in the countries of Central and Eastern Europe is still very small and will not grow substantially in the near future. This could imply that the EBRD might not find sufficient projects for investment in the first years of its operations, precisely those years which will be crucial in the transformation process. Secondly, the governments in Central and Eastern Europe have a major role to play in environmental reform projects. Furthermore, a large proportion of the infrastructure projects, essential in market-oriented economies, are not capable of privatisation in the short run or attractive for commercial bank funding.

A compromise came within reach when on 6 March 1990 the law 'on property in the USSR' was introduced in the Soviet Union. The main elements of this law, which became effective in July 1990, are: foreign citizens, as well as foreign companies may be participant in joint ventures; joint ventures may be set up as joint stock companies and foreign juridical bodies may own industrial and other property for the purpose of their business.[37] As a consequence the 'private' concept became less controversial.

Ultimately agreement was reached to replace the original concept to promote 'productive and competitive investment' by 'private and entrepreneurial initiative'. To prevent possible pressure from the recipient countries to direct EBRD lending towards entrepreneurial public enterprises the US delegation nevertheless insisted on a formal restriction on public sector support in the Agreement. And again the United States got its way. Article 11.3 (ii) of the Agreement stipulates that:

> For any country, not more than forty (40) per cent of the amount of the Bank's total committed loans, guarantees and equity investments over a period of five (5) years . . . shall be provided to the state sector.

This compromise on the scope of access to EBRD funds was not reached without resentment. In an article in *European Affairs* the Soviet delegation leader, Mr. Viktor Gerashchenko, wrote 'it is hard to assent to the EBRD's excessive focus on the private sector. It seems myopic to claim the market economy is a panacea for all evils'.[38] According to him, the fundamental criteria should be the efficiency and profitability of every single project and not exclusively the type of ownership. In this context he referred to the World Bank and the regional development banks which conduct their business with the public sector on the basis of investment profitability, not on 'dogmas of superiority of one or another type of ownership'.

Use of the European Currency Unit

The EBRD's authorized capital stock is nominated in ECU's the European Currency Unit. The ECU, created by a resolution of the European Council in December 1978 in connection with the establishment of the European Monetary System, has several functions, one of which is a unit of account for financial transactions. In this capacity its serves as a unit of account and value for all financial activities of the European Community, such as the budget, the Common Agricultural Policy, the European Development Fund and the European Investment Bank.

The ECU is a currency representing the weighted average of the currencies of the European Community members. For the weighing a basket of calculation weights in national currency units is fixed. These calculation weights in national currency units reflect their countries' relative economic weight, such as the share in the Community's aggregate gross product and in the Community's intra-trade. Multiplying these calculation weights in national currency units by the actual exchange rates gives the ECU values expressed in the Community currencies. Due to changes in the actual exchange rates, mainly as a result of occasional changes in the central rates by means of realignments, the weights change over time. Hence, the basket of calculation weights in national currency units is revised every five years. The last revision was carried out in September 1989. This opportunity was also used to include the Spanish and Portugese currencies in the system.

Country	Currency	Weights Sept 89	1 ECU average for December 1989[39]
Germany	Mark	30.1 %	2.03
France	Franc	19.0 %	6.94
United Kingdom	Pound	13.0 %	0.74
Italy	Lira	10.15%	1509.52
Netherlands	Guilder	9.4 %	2.29
Belgium	Franc	7.6 %	42.72
Spain	Peseta	5.3 %	131.20
Denmark	Krone	2.45%	7.90
Ireland	Pound	1.1 %	0.77
Greece	Drachma	0.8 %	187.22
Portugal	Escudo	0.8 %	178.14
Luxembourg	Franc	0.3 %	42.72
		100 %	
United States	Dollar		1.17
Japan	Yen		167.72

The issue of the currency or currencies that could be used for the payment of the paid-in shares was not settled without dispute. The European Community members, in particular France,[40] favoured the single use of the ECU. As Community currency this would stress the European character of the new institution, and by using one currency the EBRD would not run an exchange rate risk over its capital stock to be paid-in in equal instalments over a period of five years (article 6.1 of the Agreement). This would prevent a possible erosion of the capital, to the benefit of the recipient countries as the exchange rate risk would in this scenario be held by the shareholders themselves.[41]

However, the US delegation insisted on the use of the dollar next to the ECU, arguing that an open-ended commitment as a result of possible exchange rate risk would be unacceptable for the US Budgetary calculations[42] and that the dollar is the most widely used international currency.

The following compromise was reached. All payments obligations of a member in respect of subscription to shares in the initial capital stock or in the event of payment of the amount subscribed to the callable capital stock of the bank shall be made either in ECU, in US dollars or in Japanese yen on the basis of a fixed exchange rate, being the average rate of the relevant currency in terms of the ECU for the period from 30 September 1989 to 31 March 1990 inclusive (articles 6.3 and 6.5 of the Agreement). Thus open-ended obligations for the United States and Japan were eliminated.[43]

Presidency and location of headquarters

The preferences of the negotiating parties with regard to the nationality of the first president of the EBRD and the location of its headquarters, not surprisingly, differed considerably. However, it was clear from the start of the constitutive conference that the European Community member countries aimed at both referring to the European origin of the initiative and the European character of the new institution.

It can be argued that the EBRD should be located in one of the recipient countries. Such a decision would result in a recipient and not a 'donor' country benefiting from the creation of jobs in the administrative and support sectors of the bank's staff, from local disbursements of staff and visitors, from the demand for conference facilities, hotel accommodation and so on. The spending involved is likely to be a substantial economic impulse for the host city.[44]

Mr. Attali put the argument forward that the EBRD headquarters had 'to be close to a main financial centre, close to main sources of finance and co-ordination'.[45] Although convenient from the point of view of contacts between the institution and potential suppliers of funds, this argument can be questioned as well. Some of the regional development banks do have their headquarters in one of their recipient countries, such as the Asian Development Bank in Manila (The Philippines) and the African Development Bank in Abidjan (Ivory Coast). Neither the ADB nor the AfDB seem to suffer from the circumstance that Manila nor Abidjan is a main financial centre. Nor for that matter is Washington, hosting the headquarters of the World Bank and the Inter-American Development Bank.

Denmark was the first country officially to request to host the new institution. In a letter to President Mitterrand the Danish Prime Minister, Mr. Poul Schlueter, promoted Copenhagen as a staging post between Scandinavia and East and West recalling that Denmark did not yet host a Community institution.[46] Chancellor Franz Vranitzky of Austria made a similar plea for Vienna, arguing that Vienna will find itself virtually at the centre of the broader Europe that is opening as the Iron Curtain disintegrates. Austria, with its request for European membership pending, maintained that there is no reason why the bank has to be inside the European Community. Also in Eastern European circles there was a preference for Vienna, given its central location between East and West Europe.

Other cities, including Amsterdam, Berlin and Dublin, also presented themselves, with varying degrees of official support, as cities looking forward to host the headquarters of the EBRD. In February 1990 the British government proposed London to be home to the new institution, arguing that London already hosts more East European banks than any other European city, has the biggest Eurobond market for primary issues and is the leading equity and foreign exchange market in Europe.[47] A three-language brochure, 'European Bank for Reconstruction and Development, The Case for London', describing London's advantages as the location for the bank, was printed and circulated.[48] The US-delegation favoured Prague, but gave in to the European insistence to host the bank within the Community. According to *The Economist* in April 1990[49] London and Berlin were apparently front-runners. And of course Paris in case Mr. Attali missed the presidency as the French, as initiators, could not be left empty-handed.

For the presidency there were far less open contenders: only two. Mid January 1990 the Dutch government nominated Mr. Onno Ruding. As a former member of the board of one of the major Dutch commercial banks, former finance minister and former chairman of the influential IMF Interim Committee his candidacy received quite a few positive responses among the countries participating in the negotiations.[50] Among others the

US had made known its clear preference for a known monetary conservative like Mr. Ruding. And the British were also said to feel that support for Mr. Ruding would show their appreciation for the strong efforts by the Dutch to keep Britain from becoming completely isolated within the European Community.[51] The other candidate, for the first time publicly mentioned at the beginning of February 1990,[52] was Mr. Jacques Attali, special adviser to France's President Mitterrand and initiator of the EBRD project.

A strategy apparently emerged in a meeting of the Finance Ministers of the Group of Seven (seven major industrialised countries) preceding the IMF's Interim Committee meeting in May 1990. Of the 12 European Community member countries only Germany, France, the United Kingdom and Italy belong to the Group of Seven. In the G-7 meeting Britain withdrew its original support for Mr. Ruding in exchange for France's support for London. This coincided with indicators that Britain and France also struck the outlines of a compromise over their rankings in the quota distribution hierarchy of the IMF.[53] Consequently, in the voting, Mr. Attali won the support of 32 of the 40 countries, representing 86% of the weighted votes based on the countries' contributions to the bank's subscribed capital. And London won with 23 votes representing 70% of the weighted votes.[54]

Some of the smaller European Community countries, not involved in the decision making process of the Group of Seven, in particular the Netherlands and Belgium, objected to the outcome on procedural grounds. The presidency and location issue should not have been settled among the four Community members of the Group of Seven. But taking into account the voting majority of the Group of Seven countries in the EBRD (56%) the smaller European Community countries had to accept the French–British deal. The Netherlands showed, according to an article in the International Herald Tribune,[55] its disapproval by downgrading the level of its delegation charged with signing the Agreement establishing the Bank. Intentionally or not, a classic example of diplomatic signalling,[56] albeit for the record only. In a way the Netherlands defeated themselves by contending both for location and presidency. With a clear preference for either Amsterdam or Mr. Ruding the result might have been different.

But as usual, life goes on. Mr. Ruding accepted another job, the presidency of an employer's organisation in the Netherlands. And Amsterdam, like other European capitals, now concentrates its efforts on hosting institutions like the European Central Bank, the EC Environment Agency or the EC Trade Mark Office.[57] In the meantime another Dutchman with banking (vice chairman of merchant bank Van Lanschot) and political experience, Mr. B. le Blanc, has been appointed secretary general of the EBRD. When asked, Mr. le Blanc dismissed the suggestion that his appointment was a sort of compensation.[58] Probably rightly, given the number of management functions in the EBRD (10) and the Netherlands holding of shares (9th not counting the European Community and the European Investment Bank).

Chapter Five

The EBRD Agreement

The conference setting up the new institution, which started on 15 January 1990, resulted in an Agreement to establish the EBRD, which was signed by the contracting parties on 29 May 1990. Compared to the gestation period of similar institutions, this Agreement was drafted and agreed upon in a remarkably short time. Various factors contributed to this, such as the general view that the countries in Central and Eastern Europe, moving decisively towards democracy and market-oriented economies, should be supported as quickly as possible, as the first phase of drastic economic reforms would lead to high economic, social and political pressure. Another element was the availability of the statutes of the World Bank and other regional development and investment banks as well as the working experience with these institutions and organisations. Yet another element is the fact that the initiative was launched by a group of potential donor countries, not by a group of potential recipient countries. It took, for example, a number of Latin-American countries several years to receive the support of the United States for the establishment of the Inter-American Development Bank. The United States' reluctance was based on fears of duplicating existing institutions, such as the World Bank.[1] In this chapter those parts of the Agreement relevant in the context of the Agreement will be looked into. Particularly the mandate and structure of the EBRD. Attention will also be paid to special characteristics, such as the focus of the EBRD charter on private sector assistance and environmental protection. The chapter ends with a description of the provisions in the EBRD Agreement concerning membership.

5.1 Mandate

The general function of the bank is to borrow funds in the (international) capital markets on the best terms available and on-lend its resources to the recipient countries for purposes outlined in its charter. In this context four aspects are relevant: the purpose, functions, operations and, last but not least, the resources of the institution. These four aspects will be dealt with in this section along the respective articles in the Agreement to establish the EBRD, referring where appropriate to the various negotiating issues already described in the previous chapter.

Purpose

The purpose of the EBRD, laid down in article 1 of the Agreement, is 'in contributing to economic progress and reconstruction ... to foster the transition towards open market-oriented economies and to promote private and entrepreneurial initiative in Central and Eastern European countries committed to and applying the principles of multiparty democracy, pluralism and market economics'. In which countries is the EBRD supposed to do what?

First, the issue of the definition of recipient countries, which could alternatively be called countries of operations. In article 8.2 recipient countries are described in the same broad sense as in article 1: 'countries from Central and Eastern Europe which are proceeding steadily in the transition towards market-oriented economies and the promoting of private and entrepreneurial initiative, and which apply, by concrete steps and otherwise, the principles as set forth in Article 1 of this Agreement'. In Annex A of the Agreement, listing the countries that subscribed to the initial authorized capital stock of the EBRD, the Central and Eastern European countries which participated in the constitutive meetings and subsequently signed the Agreement are listed under the heading 'Recipient Countries'. It involves all the countries of Central and Eastern Europe, except Albania. As the heading does not read 'Possible Recipient Countries' does this imply that all these countries are, at least at the time of drafting the Agreement, proceeding steadily in the transition towards market-oriented economies and applying by concrete steps the principles of multiparty democracy and pluralism? This is not necessarily the case. As described in section 4.2 the Agreement does not contain minimum norms or time-tables to measure the required concrete progress towards market-oriented economies, multiparty democracy and pluralism. It was decided that the Board should review each recipient country's progress on decentralization, demonopolization and privatization individually to consider whether access by members to bank resources should be suspended in cases where a member might be implementing policies inconsistent with Article 1 of the Agreement. Therefore, for all participating countries from Central and Eastern Europe this implies eligibility from the start and ex-post review, with the notable exception of the Soviet Union, whose recipient status has been curtailed for three years.

Secondly, there is the twofold purpose 'to foster the transition towards open market-oriented economies' and 'to promote private and entrepreneurial initiative'. The transition towards market-oriented economies cannot succeed without simultaneous drastic political reform from a one party political system to some form of multiparty system.[2] The necessary political reform therefore forms the core of the preamble to the Agreement (see section 4.2 on the political and economic orientation of the bank). Within the broad scope of fostering the transition towards open market-oriented economies the EBRD is to focus on the private sector. The emphasis on the private sector has been dealt with in some detail in section 4.3. It may be recalled that in this context the original concept of 'productive and competitive' was changed, upon United States and British insistence, to the concept of 'private and entrepreneurial'.

Functions

The functions of the EBRD are described in article 2 of the Agreement:

> ... the Bank shall assist the recipient member countries to implement structural and sectoral economic reforms, including demonopolization, decentralization and privatization, to help their economies become fully integrated into the international economy by measures:

(i) to promote, through private and other interested investors, the establishment, improvement and expansion of productive, competitive and private sector activity, in particular small and medium sized enterprises;

(ii) to mobilize domestic and foreign capital and experienced management to the end described in (i);

(iii) to foster productive investment, including in the service and financial sectors, and in related infrastructure where that is necessary to support private and entrepreneurial initiative, thereby assisting in making a competitive environment and raising productivity, the standard of living and conditions of labour;

(iv) to provide technical assistance for the preparation, financing and implementation of relevant projects, whether individual or in the context of specific investment programmes;

(v) to stimulate and encourage the development of capital markets;

(vi) to give support to sound and economically viable projects involving more than one recipient member country;

(vii) to promote in the full range of its activities environmentally sound and sustainable development; and

(viii) to undertake such other activities and provide such other services as may further these functions.

Article 11 of the Agreement establishes the various ways in which the bank should carry out its functions, the bank's methods of operation: assisting private enterprises and certain state-owned enterprises by means of

- loans;
- investing in the equity capital and by underwriting, where other means of financing are not appropriate, the equity issue of securities;
- facilitating access to domestic and international capital markets;
- deploying Special Funds resources;
- providing technical assistance for the reconstruction and development of infrastructure, including environmental programmes, necessary for private sector development and the transition to a market-oriented economy.

The state-owned enterprises eligible for bank resources are defined in the following way: those enterprises operating competitively and moving to participation in the market economy and those in the process of transition to private ownership and control. In this regard state-owned enterprises operating competitively are described in the Agreement as those state-owned enterprises operating autonomously in a competitive market environment and subject to bankruptcy laws. The Board of Directors of the EBRD is given the authority to review, at least annually, the bank's operations and lending strategy in each recipient country in order to ensure that the purpose and functions of the bank are fully served.

The bank is bound by a range of operating principles, including that it shall

- provide not more than 40% of the total commitments to the state sector;
- not seek to obtain a controlling interest in the enterprises concerned;
- not issue guarantees for export credits nor undertake insurance activities;
- apply sound banking principles to all its operations;
- not finance an undertaking in the territory of a member objecting to such financing;
- not allow a disproportionate amount of its resources to be used for the benefit of any member;
- not undertake any financing in cases where the applicant is able to obtain sufficient financing elsewhere on terms and conditions the bank considers reasonable;

Furthermore the bank

- may where the recipient of loans or guarantees of loans is a state-owned enterprise require a public agency to guarantee the repayment of the principal etc. and
- shall charge, in addition to interest, a commission on loans made or participated in. The terms and conditions of this commission shall be determined by the Board of Directors.

In case of loans or guarantee of loans to a state-owned enterprise the EBRD may, when it appears desirable, require the member(s) in whose territory the project concerned is to be carried out to guarantee the repayment of the principle and the payment of interest and other fees and charges of the loan. The Board of Directors shall review annually the bank's practice in this matter, paying due attention to the bank's credit-worthiness (article 14.2).

The functions and methods of operation of the EBRD share

many characteristics with the World Bank group and other multilateral development/investment banks. However, apart from the political and economic orientation of its mandate, the Agreement is unique in another respect as well, i.e. the provision in the EBRD Agreement for environmental protection and the obligation to report annually on the environmental impact of its activities. Environmentally sound developments must be integrated into the full range of the bank's operations. The charters of the other multilateral development/investment banks do not contain such provisions. This distinction is not a result of the fact that Central and Eastern Europe is one of the most polluted regions in the world, but a result of the growing concern for environmental issues in general. The charters of existing institutions were drawn up decades ago, in a period in which far less attention was paid to the environment. However, in their operations they too have become increasingly sensitive to environmental concerns. For instance, as a general rule the European Investment Bank systematically scrutinises the repercussions for the environment of its activities and ensures compliance with national legislation and European Community directives on the environment. Financing for investment schemes aimed specifically at protecting or improving the environment accounted for approximately 15% of the 1989 EIB lending. Nowadays all multilateral development/investment banks report on the environmental impact of their activities.

Co-operation with other international institutions

Endorsing the French initiative to establish the EBRD the European Council stipulated that the bank should operate in consultation with the IMF and World Bank (see section 3.4). Article 2.2 of the Agreement, dealing with the co-operation of the EBRD with other international institutions, therefore reads:

> In carrying out the functions referred to in paragraph 1 of this Article, the Bank shall work in close cooperation with all its members and ... with the International Monetary Fund, the International Bank for Reconstruction and Development, the International Finance Corporation, the Multilateral Investment Guarantee Agency, and the Organisation for Economic Cooperation and Development, and shall cooperate with the United Nations and its Specialised Agencies and other related bodies, and any entity, whether public or private, concerned with the

economic development of, and investment in, Central and Eastern European countries.

The close co-operation with the IMF and the World Bank group was introduced to ensure compatibility with their activities and to benefit from their experience and expertise, as well as to ensure that recipient member countries were pursuing sound economic programmes.[3]

Resources

The resources of the EBRD consist, similarly to the resources of other development/investment banks, of

(a) the bank's own resources: paid-in capital, repayment of loans and proceeds from equity investment and income derived from loans and equity investment.

Commission and fees charged in addition to interest on loans or in underwriting the sale of securities will be kept aside as a special reserve to meet losses. The Board of Directors shall determine that all or part of it shall form part of the income of the bank. The authorised capital of the bank is ECU 10 bln, of which 30% will be paid-in in five equal yearly instalments (partly in cash, partly in promissory notes).

(b) Special Funds: the bank is authorised to accept the administration of Special Funds, contributions not related to its capital subscription, and has the power to conclude agreements of cooperation with any public or private entity or entities.

The use of these additional resources shall be consistent with the purpose and functions of the bank, and thus be used under the same restrictions as the bank's own and borrowed resources. Other regional development/investment banks have over the year acquired substantial Special Fund resources, which are used for technical co-operation and soft loan operations (very low interest rates, long grace periods and long maturities).[4]

(c) borrowed funds: the bank is authorised to borrow funds in member countries and elsewhere upon the approval of the country where the borrowing takes place and of the country in whose currency the borrowing is denominated.

Article 12.1 stipulates that the total amount of outstanding loans, equity investments and guarantees made by the bank shall not be increased at any time if, by such an increase, the total amount of its unimpaired subscribed capital (fully subscribed capital net of losses), reserves and surpluses would be exceeded. Hence a gearing ratio of 1 : 1. Not taking future reserves and surpluses into account the borrowing potential amounts ECU 7 bln, i.e. the size of the callable capital subscription. It can be expected that the EBRD will follow the EIB practice and tap resources in various European currencies, including the ECU. It is noteworthy that for the EIB the ECU share climbed into first place in 1989 with a share of 20% of the aggregate funds raised that year.[5]

5.2 Structure

The organisation and management of the EBRD resembles the structure of existing development/investment banks. All have a three-tier governing structure, consisting of a Board of Governors, a Board of Directors and a management team and staff headed by a President.

Board of Governors
The ultimate powers of the Bank are held by the Board of Governors (article 24 of the Agreement). Each member shall be represented on the Board of Governors and shall appoint one Governor and one Alternate Governor, who shall serve without remuneration from the Bank (article 23). Consequently, the EBRD has 41 Governors, 39 government officials (for a large majority of countries the Minister of Finance) and representatives of the European Community and the European Investment Bank. The Board of Governors may delegate all powers to the Board of Directors, except the power to admit new members, to suspend members, to change the authorised capital stock, to elect the Directors and the President of the Bank, to approve the general balance sheet and to amend the Agreement. The Board of Governors will hold annual meetings and, on the basis of specified quorums, ad hoc meetings on their own initiative or on the request of the Board of Directors.

Board of Directors

The Board of Directors consists of 23 members (article 26), of whom

- 11 are elected by the Governors representing the 12 European Community countries, the European Community and the European Investment Bank (representing 51% of the authorised capital stock),
- 4 are elected by the Governors representing the 7 Central and Eastern European countries (11.9%),
- 4 are elected by the Governors representing the 11 non-EC European countries, including Israël (11.3%) and
- 4 are elected by the Governors representing the 9 non-European countries (24.2%).

The Board of Governors may increase or decrease the size of the Board of Directors or revise its composition (article 26.3). Directors must be nationals of member countries and no member can be represented by more than one Director. Directors hold office for a term of three years and may be re-elected. A list of the constituencies formed and the names and previous functions of the Directors appointed is given in appendix 5.

The Board of Directors shall be responsible for the direction of the general operations of the bank and shall according to article 27:

(i)   prepare the work of the Board of Governors;
(ii) in conformity with the general directions of the Board of Governors, establish policies and take decisions concerning loans, guarantees, investments in equity capital, borrowing by the Bank, the furnishing of technical assistance, and other operations of the Bank;
(iii) submit the audited accounts for each financial year for approval of the Board of Governors at each annual meeting; and
(iv) approve the budget of the Bank.

These powers are to a large extent similar to those assigned to the Directors in other investment/development banks. The voting provisions have been dealt with in chapter 3. The quorum requirement for meetings of the Board of Directors is a majority of the Directors, representing not less than two-thirds of the voting power.

During the negotiations the issue was raised whether the Directors should be resident (and hence on the pay-roll of the bank) or non-resident as in the case of the European Investment Bank. The majority of the European Community countries originally favoured a non-resident Board in order to economize on the bank's expenditure. However, in the end it was decided to have a resident Board, albeit that for the year 1991 the number of Alternates and supporting Board staff paid for by the bank would be limited.

Management

The chief of the staff of the bank, responsible for the organisation, appointment and dismissal of staff is the President of the bank, elected by the Board of Governors by a majority of the number of Governors representing not less than half of the total voting power of the members. The President conducts, under the direction of the Board of Directors, the current business of the bank. The President holds office for a term of four years and may be re-elected (article 30). One or more Vice-Presidents shall be appointed by the Board of Directors on the recommendation of the President (article 31). In appointing staff the President shall pay due regard to recruitment on a wide geographical basis among members of the Bank and shall give men and women equal opportunities in the recruitment process and in terms of service, training, promotion and career development.[6]

5.3 Membership

Article 3 of the Agreement establishing the EBRD concerns membership. It stipulates that membership shall be open to (1) European countries and (2) non-European countries which are members of the International Monetary Fund, as well as (3) the European Community and the European Investment Bank. The condition of IMF membership can be traced back to the resolution of the European Council endorsing the EBRD initiative in December 1989, stating that the new institution will work in consultation with the IMF and World Bank. The general policy line adopted by the G-24 countries (OECD members) that assistance to Central and Eastern Europe, apart from emergency and humanitarian aid, should only be offered to those countries implementing structural adjustment policies agreed upon and in co-operation with the IMF could not be applied as the Soviet Union is not yet a (full) member of this Bretton Woods institution. It could be argued that making IMF membership compulsory for all members with the explicit exception of the Soviet Union and possibly Albania would have made more sense than the chosen limitation of IMF membership to non-European countries, which can only join the bank as donors, and cannot become recipient members of the new institution. But there might be a specific reason for the formula adopted: namely to avoid difficulties that could arise in the event of a membership application by Taiwan. Taiwan, not being a member of the IMF/World Bank group, showed its interest in the bank by indicating that it would provide financial support for the bank's programmes for technical assistance, training and advisory services.[7]

The countries and institutions that signed the establishing Agreement could become members (a party to the Agreement) by depositing an instrument of ratification, acceptance or approval until one year after the date of its entry into force. Countries that did not sign the establishing Agreement may, within the mentioned restrictions, be admitted upon affirmative vote of not less than two-thirds of the Governors, representing not less than three-quarters of the total voting power of the members (article 3.2). Institutions that did not sign the establishing Agreement cannot be admitted, unless the Agreement is amended in this respect. Membership will be limited to the European Community and the European Investment Bank. The World Bank, IFC and the three regional development banks do not allow institutions to be admitted as members. It was, however, not intended that the membership of the European Community and the European Investment Bank of the EBRD would be used as a precedent for them or other institutions to become members of other organisations or other banks.[8]

If a member fails to fulfil any of its obligations to the bank, the bank may suspend its membership. The suspended member will cease to be a member one year from the date of its suspension unless a decision is taken to restore the member to good standing (article 37). Any member may withdraw from the bank at any time by transmitting a notice to this effect in writing to the bank (article 38).

5.4 Basic documents

Before concluding this chapter on the EBRD Agreement, it should be mentioned that there are two annexes attached to it, dealing with (a) the initial subscriptions to the authorised capital stock for prospective members (reproduced in appendix 2) and (b) the procedures for the election of its Directors. Furthermore there are two other documents that form part of the EBRD's basic documents. The first one is the letter by the head of the Soviet delegation regarding the preparedness to limit the Soviet access to the bank's resources (reproduced in appendix 3). The second one is a report by the conference chairman, summarising certain general understandings with regard to the text of the Agreement which needed to be recorded but which were not suitable for the articles. This report is reproduced in appendix V of Ibrahim F.I. Shihata's book, *The European Bank for Reconstruction and Development / a comparative analysis of the constituent agreement* (London, 1990, pp. 166–180).

Chapter Six

The Preparatory Phase

In this chapter attention will be paid to the period between the signing of the Agreement on 29 May 1990 and the date that the Agreement entered into force, 15 April 1991, the date that the EBRD became operational. It was intended to do as much preparatory work as possible in order to enable the Governors to approve the commencement of the bank's operations soon after the Agreement's entry into force. To this end the President-designate received a mandate to form a transitional team[1] seconded by member countries, the European Investment Bank as well as a small number of consultants financed from the working capital (ECU 10 million) by means of a loan from the European Investment Bank. By October 1990 the transitional team of experts (legal, corporate finance, development lending etc.) had grown to 26. According to Mr. Attali the bank's envisaged staff would number 200 to 250.[2] Others came up with higher numbers, more in line with the staff employed by similar institutions like the IFC (550) and the EIB (750). Mr. Attali and his (growing) transitional team started their preparatory work in Paris, in accommodation paid for by the French government. In August 1990 the team moved to temporary offices in the City of London, financed by the British government.

In this chapter three topics will be highlighted, the two monthly follow-up conferences by the shareholders, the ratification proceedings and the inauguration of the bank, which ended the preparatory phase on 15 April 1991.

6.1 The follow-up conferences

The first of the two monthly follow-up conferences, dealing in particular with financial projections, by-laws, rules and procedures for the Board of Governors and Board of Directors, and with staff regulations, was held on 18 and 19 July 1990. The meeting took place in London, the British government taking over the role of host from the French government. The conference was chaired by the EBRD's President-designate, Mr. Attali. Representatives from all future founding members attended the conference. During this first follow-up meeting a sharp confrontation developed between Mr. Attali on the one side and almost all delegations on the other. This was attributed to differing views on some issues at stake, among others Mr. Attali wanting to make the bank as 'Presidential' as possible by concentrating power on himself as President rather than leaving authority for approving policy and loans with the Board of executive Directors from member countries.[3] The reluctance of Mr. Attali to accept changes proposed by shareholders apparently contributed to the problem as well as his brusque handling of the discussions.[4]

The second conference in October 1990 proved to be more constructive and more productive. The atmosphere had changed from confrontation to co-operation. The President-designate this time appeared to be sensitive to the ideas and concerns of shareholders. During this meeting a draft framework for a business plan and a two year financial projection paper, prepared by the transitional team were discussed. Privatisation, the creation of private financial institutions, infrastructure development and technical assistance and training were listed as the key areas for early attention.[5] The financial projections showed a net loss for the bank of up to US $96 million in 1991 and, in the best case scenario, a profit of US $41 million in 1992.[6] The income would come mainly from interest earnings on cash payments for shares, commitment fees on undisbursed loans and interest rate margins charges on loans. Furthermore, the basic principles of the salary and benefits structure for the bank's staff and Board were discussed. Finally, the delegations were informed that the bank had launched an international design competition for the bank's logo, which 'will form the basis of the Bank's visual identity'.[7]

The third follow-up conference took place in January 1991. The discussions focused on draft policy papers on the initial action programme, technical assistance and operational, financial, environmental and human rights policies. The shareholders furthermore agreed upon a list of initial investment priorities,[8] being

• private sector development, privatisation and restructuring of private enterprises;
• financial sector reform, setting up venture capital and mutual funds as well as the establishment of financial intermediaries, including private banks and
• energy efficiency, environmental and infrastructure projects, telecommunications.

Also during this conference the organisational structure of the bank was discussed. According to information made public by the Bank in March 1991 it was envisaged that the institution would have two operational departments, Merchant Banking and Development Banking, and eight other units: Finance, Personnel and Administration, Evaluation, Chief Economist's Office, General Counsel's Office, Secretary General's Office, Press and Communications and Internal Audit. A synopsis of the role of the mentioned departments and offices is attached in appendix 6.

The game of musical chairs by the various Vice-Presidential candidates started early. The first candidate, publicly in the picture, was Mr. Ernest Stern, one of the three senior World Bank Vice-Presidents. Mr. Stern, a US citizen, was seen as eminently qualified.[9] But he rejected the offer. Others did seize the opportunity, such as Mr. Miklos Nemeth, the last communist Prime Minister of Hungary, who has played an important role in furthering political reform in Hungary and under whose government Hungary opened its border to Austria facilitating massive emigration of GRD citizens to West Germany (Vice-President of Personnel & Administration). Mr. Mario Sarcinelli who in his capacity as Director General of the Italian Ministry of Finance headed the Italian delegation in the constitutive meetings was nominated Vice-President of Development Banking. Mr. Anders Ljungh, head of international operations at the Swedish Svenska Handelsbanken accepted the Vice-Presidency of Finance and

Mr. Manfred Abelein, a German politician, was nominated Vice-President of Project Evaluation, bringing the total number of Vice-Presidents to five. Mr. John Flemming, chief economic adviser of the Bank of England, was designated to become the EBRD's Chief Economist.[10]

However, the nominee for the Vice-Presidency of Merchant Banking could not be presented to the first Board meeting following the inaugural ceremony in April 1991. It was expected that an American would be nominated, for political reasons as well as the fact that the United States was the largest shareholder of the bank. The reasons for the delay were said to be twofold: firstly that those candidates suggested to Mr. Attali did not, in his view, live up to the high standards he had set, and secondly that some of the candidates who interested Mr. Attali considered it impossible to work for him.[11] On 6 June 1991 the EBRD announced the appointment of Mr. Ronald Freeman, a top investment banker, head of European investment banking at Salomon Brothers, as First Vice-President, Merchant Banking. Asked about Mr. Attali's supposedly autocratic management style and suggestions that he would be difficult to work with, Mr. Freeman said: 'I have survived on Wall Street for nearly 18 years. Difficult and mercurial figures are a common form of life there'.[12]

The fourth follow-up conference was held in March 1991, a few weeks in advance of the inauguration, scheduled for 15 April 1991. During this meeting the draft resolutions for the first meeting of the Board of Governors were discussed.

6.2 Ratification

The Agreement establishing the EBRD was signed in Paris on 29 May 1990 and subsequently deposited with the Government of France, which had agreed to be the depository for this agreement. The Agreement stipulates that it shall enter into force when signatories, whose subscriptions represent not less than two-thirds of the initial authorised capital, including at least two countries from Central and Eastern Europe, have ratified, accepted or approved the agreement (article 62). This shall be done not later than 31 March 1991 (article 61).

When the Agreement enters into force the Board of Governors shall hold their first meeting within 60 days. At this meeting the

Board of Governors shall elect the President, the Directors and make arrangements for determining the date of commencement of the Bank's operations (article 63). If by 31 March 1991 the Agreement has not entered into force the Depository may convene a conference of interested prospective members to determine the future course of action.

The first shareholders to ratify the Agreement was France, the initiator of the EBRD project. The 'Assemblée Nationale' approved the Agreement on 22 June 1990 and the 'Sénat' on 28 June 1990. On both occasions the Communist party abstained from voting.[13] The party apparently did not yet approve of the changes in Central and Eastern Europe towards market economies leading to the dismantling of the heritage of socialism. By the end of March 1991 shareholders representing 75% of the initial authorised capital had ratified the agreement,[14] exceeding the mandatory two-thirds level.

6.3 Inauguration

The inaugural ceremony was held in London on 15 April 1991. The proceedings took place in the office building of the International Maritime Organization, a United Nations affiliate, the only multilateral governmental institution having its head-quarters in London. About half of the founding countries were represented by their respective Heads of State or Government. The delegations of most of the other countries were headed by their Ministers of Finance, participating in their capacity as Governors of the bank. Dutch Finance Minister Mr. Kok was elected chairman of the Board of Governors.

Keynote addresses were delivered by the British Prime Minister John Major, as head of the host country, French President François Mitterrand, who launched the initiative that evolved into the establishment of the new bank and Mr. Jacques Attali, the President of the EBRD.

The British Prime Minister called the idea of setting up the EBRD an example of international co-operation at its timeliest, most constructive best. Referring to the responsibility given in July 1989 to the European Community for co-ordinating Western aid to Central and Eastern Europe he said 'it is natural that the first move to establish a new bank should have been made by the European Community . . . we had to be as bold as the people in Eastern Europe we were trying to help'. The Prime Minister mentioned that once the course of action was agreed two vitally important decisions were of special interest to Britain: where to locate the headquarters and who to appoint as President? 'I think partners made the right choices . . . London is the natural home for the EBRD. It is already home to more than 500 banks, Europe's greatest financial centre.' Mr. Major went on to stress the explicit political aim of the bank and its focus on the private sector and expressed the hope that in the years to come London will have a central role in the successful economic development of Central and Eastern Europe, a role reinforced by the presence of a flourishing EBRD.

After the rather practical speech of the British Prime Minister, French President Mitterrand embarked on a more philosophical line, the emergence of a new European order, a united Europe.

Mr. Attali stated that his intention was 'to listen to what you have to say and understand your vision of the part the Bank can play in the new continental architecture'. Furthermore he highlighted the specificity and uniqueness of the bank, being the first institution of the post-cold-war period, of a united Europe and of the new world order. In this context Mr. Attali stated that:

- the institution brings together former adversaries (political, economic and ideological); it will help to strengthen peaceful relations between them by promoting democracy and the market economy;
- it is the first institution of which all European countries are full equal members, in rights and duties; in this way it will become the natural forum for the great debates leading up to the formation of a continental economic space;
- it will demonstrate that nowadays no economic development is possible without respect for human rights, in the hope that this lesson will be heard far beyond the confines of Europe.

He concluded his address in the following, remarkable way: The European Bank 'will then be worthy of all the visionaries who have looked forward to this throughout the centuries: from Spinoza to Tolstoy, from Hobbes to Voltaire, from Goethe to Kafka. Above all, it will be the culmination of centuries of struggle against barbarity and dictatorship, in the camps of Auschwitz and the Gulag, and in the streets of Madrid, Paris and Prague. It will be the heir of von Staufenberg and Moulin, Benes and Masaryk, Garcia Lorca and Sakharov, who died with this vision in mind. I would like, personally, to dedicate this day to their memory, trusting that we may at last prove worthy of their hopes and that one day 700 million Europeans may unite in a single ideal of peace, tolerance and light'.

The inaugural ceremony was followed by the first meeting of the Board of Governors, modelled on the annual meetings of the Governors of the IMF and the World Bank. A dozen Governors took the floor. The US Secretary of the Treasury, Mr. Brady, pointed out that 'the United States stands ready to help transform the nations of Central and Eastern Europe into growing democratic market economies. . . . The EBRD has a central role to play in turning these aspirations into reality. . . . The private sector emphasis, which is also a legal requirement, was a critical element of U.S. support for the Bank. . . . We believe strongly that the EBRD's focus should be private sector development and the financing of infrastructure which directly supports private sector activity'. Mr. Brady used the opportunity to stress the role of the Directors. 'We, the shareholders, have a responsibility to provide the Bank, through our Directors, with clear political guidance. The Directors, as personal representatives of the Governors, must play a key role in developing the focus of the EBRD. The Board of Directors, therefore, should be fully involved and informed. . . . We do not view the activity of the Board as an advisory one, but, instead, as a critical element of the Bank's operations'.

The Soviet Governor, Mr. Gerashchenko, Chairman of the Gosbank, in his turn, recalled that the negotiating process has been full of compromise and concessions and mentioned the unique position of the Soviet Union in the EBRD, i.e. the total volume of credit and other services received by the Soviet Union should not exceed the size of its paid-in capital during the first three years. He expressed the hope that 'our determination to implement reforms will allow this clause to be eliminated in the near future', to which he added that 'already now one can witness a growing understanding of this issue in the West'. He obviously referred to the appeal, among others made by a senior German Ministry of Finance official, to abolish the credit restrictions imposed on the Soviet Union as soon as possible.[15] Mr.

Attali is also said to be campaigning for an easing of the restrictions imposed on the Soviet Union.[16]

Obviously the bank wants to play a key role in the restructuring of the Soviet economy and puts a lot of effort in establishing this role. The first country action programme and projects made public by the bank consequently concerned the Soviet Union and not reform front-runners such as Poland or Hungary. The programme was submitted in the beginning of June to the G-7 nations and Mr. Gorbachev.[17] The projects involved concerned an agreement with the State Bank of the Soviet Union to help set up a new bank and an agreement to be an adviser to the Moscow Council for Privatisation.[18]

Returning to the inaugural meeting, the Governors elected Mr. Attali to become the first President of the EBRD, elected the Directors and approved the resolutions prepared during the transitional period. The first meeting of the Governors was followed by the first meeting of the Board of Directors. The first policy paper endorsed by the Directors was the paper on 'Operational Challenges and Priorities: Initial Orientations', providing an initial view of the operational challenges and priorities facing the new institution, a first framework for its operations. This policy paper is reproduced in appendix 7.

Chapter Seven

The EBRD in Perspective

In earlier chapters, the idea of establishing a new international financial institution to assist the countries in Central and Eastern Europe in their transition towards more market-oriented economies was outlined within the political and economic context of the initiative during the second half of 1989. In the following parts the negotiation process leading to the Agreement to establish the EBRD and subsequently to the inauguration of the EBRD, was examined step-by-step. In this final chapter the emergence of the EBRD will be looked at in retrospect as well as in perspective. First, the original idea will be compared to the outcome of the negotiations. What did the various participating countries envisage and to what extent did they manage to influence the outcome of the negotiations? Then attention will be paid to the role the new institution can play in relation to the overall challenges facing the countries in Central and Eastern Europe in their transition processes. To what extent is the EBRD capable of addressing vital needs of the recipient countries? Finally, the kind of activities upon which the EBRD should concentrate and the abilities it should demonstrate in order to become, within the scope of its mandate, an effective tool to help bring about and sustain the transition towards democracy and market economics in Central and Eastern Europe, will be examined.

7.1 The creation of a new kind of institution

At the outset France envisaged the creation of a bank which would finance major projects in Central and Eastern Europe. Not only projects in the leading reforming countries, Poland and Hungary, but also in other countries of the region, including notably the Soviet Union. The bank was to be established and managed by European countries, and would raise resources on the international capital markets for the financing of large-scale projects in the field of agriculture, transport, telecommunications and finance. It was to be an additional channel to assist countries in Central and Eastern Europe in their transition from centrally planned economies into more market-oriented economies.

In essence, the original idea was to create a regional investment/development bank for Europe, like those established to assist the less developed countries in Africa, Asia and Central and South America. By creating such an institution it would, among others, be possible to include the Soviet Union in the Western assistance programme: the Soviet Union was not a member of the IMF/World Bank group nor was it eligible for the 1989–1990 G–24 assistance geared at reform front-runners in Central and Eastern Europe.

As to the issue of participation of non-European (donor) countries in the new institution the French were ambiguous. On the one hand they favoured a European institution, on the other hand it was realised that the more donor countries that participated, the greater the amount of resources that would become available. The European Council, endorsing the general idea in December 1989, settled the membership issue by inviting other countries to join, in particular the other member countries of the OECD. Thus the participation of the United States and Japan, among others, was requested.

Such a regional development/investment bank as this would, to a considerable extent, duplicate the World Bank's mandate, as could be said of the mandates and activities of the existing regional development banks. Although fear of duplication did delay the establishment of the first such bank, the Inter-American Development Bank,[1] these institutions have since established their right to exist. Consequently, a Central/Eastern European Development Bank, structured along the lines of the existing regional development banks is also feasible and can be argued in the following way: (a) competition, even among bureaucracies, is healthy,[2] (b) it makes sense to have a regional institution that can attract strong support from neighbouring countries and that generates special expertise concerning the region[3] and (c) it may help to keep financial assistance to Central and Eastern Europe separate from financial assistance to the Third World (see section 3.4).

The EBRD, however, did not emerge as a traditional regional development bank. During the mandate negotiations the original idea evolved into the creation of a different kind of institution: an institution capable of lending to states (as does the World Bank and the traditional regional development banks) as well as lending to the private sector (like the International Finance Corporation). The emphasis was placed on lending to the private sector. Lending to the state sector has been limited to a maximum of 40% of the amount of the EBRD's loans, guarantees and equity investments (article 11.3). There are clear advantages of having a single management lending to both the private and public sector: as co-operation between different departments within one institution should be less difficult than co-operation between different institutions.

Furthermore, a new concept has been introduced at the level of multilateral institutions because the EBRD obtained a political and economic orientation in its mandate. By not taking only economic and social feasibility considerations into account, as is the policy of other international financial institutions such as the World Bank, and by introducing into the mandate of the new institution the requirement of a commitment to and application of the principles of multiparty democracy, pluralism and market economics by recipient countries, a new departure was achieved.

It may be recalled that democracy and a market-oriented economy are not conditions required of states seeking assistance of regional development banks or the Bretton Woods institutions. Those charters specifically prohibit the institutions from being influenced by political considerations and the IMF covenant does take into account aspects of a non-market economy. That is why for instance Romania and China could obtain membership.

The political and economic orientation was introduced at the insistence of a large majority of the Western participants in the negotiations, restating at a multilateral level the conditional approach adopted by them on their own bilateral assistance arrangements to reforming Central and Eastern European countries. These countries were consistent in making assistance only available for serious reformers, and by accepting this direction, the Central and Eastern European participants were serious about their commitment to democracy and market economics. But definitions of democracy, pluralism and market economics vary widely. As has been outlined in section 4.2, it is likely that in the course of this political and economic orientation, sooner or later, tough discussions and difficult decisions will emerge.

The following table gives an overview of the postions France, the EC countries in general and the United States, originally took in the negotiations regarding the main issues, including the new concept mentioned above. The last column of the table presents the outcome that the negotiations produced after debate:

Issues	France	EC majority	US	Outcome
• *membership*:				
Soviet Union	yes	yes	no	yes
US/Japan		yes		yes
• *economic orientation*:				
commitment	yes	yes	yes	yes
actual implementation	no	yes	yes	yes
• *political orientation*:				
commitment	yes	yes	yes	yes
actual implementation	no	mixed	mixed	yes
• *restricted lending to*:				
public sector	no	mixed	yes	yes
Soviet Union	no	mixed	yes	yes
• *capital*:				
size in ECU bln	15	mixed	5	10
EC majority share	yes	yes	yes	yes
use of ECU only	yes	mixed	no	no
• *preference for*:				
presidency	Attali	mixed	banker	Attali
location of headquarters		mixed	Prague	London

As has been outlined in the last section of chapter 3, in managing to convince their Community partners to accept the idea of establishing a new institution, the French can be considered as having achieved a remarkable success. The overall outcome of the negotiations is also a remarkable success for the United States and in its wake Britain and Japan on the one hand and the Soviet Union on the other. Although the United States had encouraged Western Europe to take the lead with regard to Western assistance to Central and Eastern Europe, once invited to join the constitutive EBRD conference, the United States made it clear that such a policy could not be extended to the Soviet Union. Supported by Japan, and by the fact that European Community countries held different views on the purpose and functions of the new institution, the United States managed to dominate the negotiations in this respect. In good hegemonic tradition the United States frequently set down the terms and scope of the involvement, if any, of the Soviet Union. The Soviet Union, albeit reluctantly, accepted the political and economic orientation as well as a temporary restriction of its recipient status: a clear proof that it was prepared to compromise to a considerable extent in order to join the international financial community.

7.2 What does Central/Eastern Europe need?

The transition towards democracy and market-oriented economies is first and foremost an affair of the peoples and governments of the Central and Eastern countries themselves. Now that the Soviet Union has moved its policy away from regional dominance, the countries in Central and Eastern Europe are free to pursue their own policies. They are free to opt for democracy and market economics. In case they and the Soviet Union do so, one of the main and perhaps most important factors determining the success of the transition process is the abolition of the policy of isolationalism, which would lead to the integration of those states into the world economy. This can be facilitated by endorsing membership of those countries in existing international institutions, both political and economic, and by opening up Western markets to exports of goods, services and labour from Central and Eastern Europe.

All Central and Eastern European countries, except for the Soviet Union and Albania, have in the meantime acquired membership of the IMF and World Bank group and have become contracting parties in the GATT. The Soviet Union obtained observer status in the GATT in May 1990, after a waiting period of four years. Furthermore it will, following the discussions during the G–7 economic summit in London in July 1991, be able to obtain a special relationship with the Bretton Woods institutions. The Soviet Union's EBRD Governor has, quite modestly, stated that his country recognises the significant role the EBRD can play to facilitate its membership in other multilateral financial organisations. But is this necessary? Membership of the IMF and World Bank is basically open to all countries. Notwithstanding the expectations expressed by the Soviet Governor of the bank mentioned earlier, the EBRD should have no role to play in this context. Many of the arguments used against Soviet membership lose their value when compared to the acceptance of China in the Bretton Woods institutions. If the Western countries, in particular the United States, are serious about integration of the Soviet Union in the world economy, they should endorse its full membership in the IMF and World Bank without further delay. A view the Soviets have come round to by applying for IMF membership in July 1991.

The EBRD can play a role in facilitating the establishment of association agreements between the European Community and some of the countries of Central and Eastern Europe, notably Poland, Hungary and Czechoslovakia. Apart from the political importance of such agreements for the governments of these countries, the private sector in these countries can only embark on sustained growth where there are ample export opportunities. It can therefore be expected that the bank will stress the need for access to the world economy and, given the proximity, to the European Community in particular. The majority share of the European Community countries (including Community and EIB) in the EBRD as well as the presence of the European Community and the countries in Central and Eastern Europe in its Board of Directors make the EBRD a potential channel of communication on this topic.

Next to the integration of Central and Eastern Europe in the world economy debt relief is a priority for a number of countries in Central and Eastern Europe. Substantive debt relief is essential for a successful transition to Poland, Bulgaria, Yugoslavia and Hungary. At the beginning of 1991 Western governments did embark on a decisive policy by forgiving about half of the US$33 billion debt (to a large extent interest arrears) owed

by Poland.[4] It can be argued that other non-communist governments in Central and Eastern Europe, implementing drastic
reform policies, should be granted such a relative clean start as
well. Debt relief falls beyond the mandate of the EBRD. However, its analytical abilities and potential for gearing up new
lending can contribute to the overall management of the debt
problem in the region concerned.

In the field of knowledge transfer by means of training, technical assistance, technology transfer, institution building and
policy advice the EBRD can and should play an important role,
confined as its mandate is to the region concerned. As the bulk
of these activities can hardly be implemented on a commercial
basis the bank should be amply supplied with Special Funds and
financial support for its programmes for technical assistance.
During the bank's inaugural meeting one country, Norway,
signed an agreement which provided for a grant of 5 million
kroner (£430,000) to the bank and 7 other countries indicated
that they will support the bank in this way.[5] More countries may
follow suit.

After matters concerning integration, substantive debt relief
and knowledge transfer, a key element of the Western official
assistance to the transformation process is support for the private sector, the core of the mandate of the EBRD. In this area
the EBRD is equipped to undertake a whole range of activities.
The methods of operations have been described in chapter 5. It
is beyond the scope of this analysis to investigate whether the
initial priorities set by the bank are in line with the most urgent
needs, an evaluation that can only be made in a few years time.
One of the aspects that can be highlighted in advance is the division between loans and investments in equity capital. In the first
years loans will, on average, result in higher returns and will,
again on average, be more secure than equity investments. On a
commercial basis therefore loans should be preferred to equity
investments. However, private companies in Central and Eastern
Europe will benefit more from resources in the form of equity
capital than from loans. The EBRD should therefore allocate a
substantial share of its activities to equity investment and thus
be allowed, if necessary, to run losses for a period of years. By
doing so the bank will not acquire reserves and hence additional room to manoeuvre in the short term, but this will not

hamper its operating capacity as its capital subscription and borrowing capacity is likely to be sufficient for at least, say, the first five years.

7.3 What role can the EBRD play?

Opinions on the need to create the EBRD and on the role the bank can play vary widely. The preceding analysis on the origin and mandate of the institution leads me to the conclusion that the bank has a distinct, important role to play in the integration of Europe, the integration of Central and Eastern Europe into the international financial system and in the establishment of the private sector in recipient countries. Success in these tasks would benefit both recipients and donors. The EBRD is however not a unique institution in the sense that it is the only institution which contributes to these important objectives. There are others as has been outlined earlier. Nor can the EBRD at this stage be qualified as the most important institution in this respect. Independently of which institution may take the leading role in these activities careful attention must be paid to co-ordination among donors, recipients and international financial institutions in order to avoid unproductive duplication of activities and to achieve the best overall results.

Some of the critics of the bank have questioned the need to establish the EBRD. They argue that it will perform functions that are already covered by other international financial institutions such as the World Bank, the International Finance Corporation and the European Investment Bank. Indeed, the methods of operations of the EBRD are a combination of those of the mentioned institutions. But one should take into account that (a) by creating a new institution an additional amount of ECU 10 bln is made available (an amount not likely to be added to the capital of the other institutions), (b) the Soviet Union is not included in the programme and project mandate of the IMF/ World Bank group nor in the EIB activities in Central and Eastern Europe, and (c) lending to both the private and public sector by one institution is advantageous.

Some of its staunch supporters, on the other hand, stress the uniqueness of the EBRD. They argue that it is the first institution of the new world order, as well as the first institution with a political and economic oriented mandate. Indeed, co-operation in the EBRD will help to strengthen the peaceful relations between former adversaries: but so do other institutions and conferences such as the Council of Europe and the CSCE. Furthermore, on-lending of resources on commercial terms, albeit the best terms available, can hardly be called sharing of vital interests, demonstrated in the past by the European Coal and Steel Community (see section 3.3. Common house for Europe). A new world order can only be created in the case of vital interests being shared. An important step could be made by endorsing the future membership of Central and Eastern European countries in the European Community and perhaps even NATO.

The political and economic oriented mandate of the EBRD is indeed a unique feature. Although the lending policy of the IMF/World Bank group is, de facto, increasingly affected by political events, it will be interesting to see whether the EBRD experience in particular on political conditionality will lead to fundamental re-thinking in other international financial institutions.[6]

It is too early to assess the result of the EBRD action programme. If however the EBRD is to be a tool to help sustain the move to democracy and market economics it will need to demonstrate an ability to (a) produce effective analysis of the problems facing the private sector in Central and Eastern Europe; (b) identify actions which will unblock existing barriers in the transition process; (c) demonstrate a flexible and responsive approach within the limits of its mandate, and (d) find an acceptable combination of traditional public sector concerns regarding infrastructure with private sector approaches to investment banking. An important task lies ahead!

Appendix 1

List of names and functions of the heads of the delegations participating in the EBRD constitutive conference

European Community

Belgium	Mr. B. Snoy	– Chef de Cabinet Ministère des Finances
Denmark	Mr. N-J. Nehring	– Conseiller Special Service du Premier Ministre
France	Mr. J-C. Trichet	– Directeur du Trésor Ministère des Finances
F.R. of Germany	Mr. E. Pieske	– Deputy Director Ministère des Finances
Greece	Mr. A. Raphael	– Amassadeur de Grèce en France
Ireland	Mr. M. Somers	– Secrétaire général chargé de l'administration de la Dette Publique
Italy	Mr. M. Sarcinelli	– Directeur Général du Trésor Ministère des Finances
Luxembourg	Mr. Y. Mersch	– Directeur du Trésor Ministère du Trésor
Netherlands	Mr. C. Maas	– Directeur du Trésor Ministère des Finances
Portugal	Mr. C.S. Costa	– Coordinateur des Affaires économiques et financières à la représéntation auprès de la CEE

Spain	Mr. M. Conthe	- Directeur Général du Trésor Ministère des Finances
United Kingdom	Mr. N. Wicks	- Second Permanent Secretary Treasury
Eur. Community	Mr. D. Williamson	- Secrétaire général de la Commission
Eur. Inv. Bank	Mr. E.G. Bröder	- Président

Other European countries

Austria	Mr. H. Luschin	- Adviser to Director General Ministère Fédéral des Finances
Cyprus	Mr. M. Erotocritos	- Directeur Général du Ministère des Finances
Finland	Mr. L. Fagernas	- Directeur Général Adjoint Ministère des Affaires Etrangères
Iceland	Mr. J. Sigurdsson	- Ministre du Commerce
Israël	Mr. M. Bruno	- Gouverneur de la Banque d'Israël
Liechtenstein	Mr. R. Marxer	- Chef de l'Office des Affaires Etrangères
Malta	Mr. J. Licari	- Ambassadeur de Malte à Bruxelles
Norway	Mr. S. Svedman	- Secrétaire d'Etat Ministère des Affaires Etrangères
Sweden	Mr. G. Lund	- Secrétaire d'Etat Ministère des Finances
Switzerland	Mr. F. Blankart	- Secrétaire d'Etat Office Fédéral des Affaires Economiques Extérieures
Turkey	Mr. T. Altan	- General Director of Treasury and Foreign Trade Prime Ministry

Recipient countries

Bulgaria	Mr. M. Dinev	- First Deputy Minister of Finance
Czecho-slovakia	Mr. V. Klaus	- Ministre des Finances
German Dem. Rep.	Mr. W. Polze	- Président de la Banque Allemande du Commerce Extérieur
Hungary	Mr. F. Bartha	- State Secretary and President of National Bank of Hungary
Poland	Mr. A. Olechowski	- First Deputy President of National Bank of Poland
Romania	Mr. S. Ghencea	- Deputy Chairman of the Bank for Agriculture and Food Industry
Soviet Union	Mr. V. Gerashchenko	- Chairman of the Board USSR State Bank
Yugoslavia	Mr. B. Skapin	- Assistant Secretary Federal Secretariat for Finance

Non-European countries

| Australia | Mr. R. Simes | - Ministre aux Affaires Economiques et Financières auprès de l'Ambassade |
| Canada | Mr. D. Dodge | - Associate Deputy Minister Department of Finance |

Egypt	Mr. A. Sidky	– Ambassadeur d'Egype à Paris
Japan	Mr. M. Utsumi	– Vice-Ministre des Affaires Internationales au Ministère des Finances
South Korea	Mr. Y-S. Lee	– Assistant Minister Ministry of Finance
Mexico	Mr. A. Gurria	– Secrétaire d'Etat aux Finances chargé des Affaires de Financement International
Morocco	Mr. M. Dairi	– Directeur du Trésor Ministère des Finances
New Zealand	Mr. G. Wheeler	– Conseiller Economique auprès de l'Ambassade
United States	Mr. D. Mulford	– Under Secretary for International Affairs Department of Treasury

Source: EBRD/Réunion des chefs de délégation, liste des participants, Paris, 8 et 9 avril 1990.

Appendix 2

EBRD initial capital stock subscriptions by Agreement signatories

	Capital Subscription in ECU million
European Community	
Belgium	228.000
Denmark	120.000
France	851.750
F.R. of Germany	851.750
Greece	65.000
Ireland	30.000
Italy	851.750
Luxembourg	20.000
Netherlands	248.000
Portugal	42.000
Spain	340.000
United Kingdom	851.750
European Community	300.000
European Investment Bank	300.000
Other European countries	
Austria	228.000
Cyprus	10.000
Finland	125.000
Iceland	10.000
Israël	65.000
Liechtenstein	2.000
Malta	1.000
Norway	125.000

Sweden	228.000
Switzerland	228.000
Turkey	115.000

Recipient countries

Bulgaria	79.000
Czechoslovakia	128.000
German Democratic Republic	155.000
Hungary	79.000
Poland	128.000
Romania	48.000
Soviet Union	600.000
Yugoslavia	128.000

Non-European countries

Australia	100.000
Canada	340.000
Egypt	10.000
Japan	851.750
South Korea	65.000
Mexico	30.000
Morocco	10.000
New Zealand	10.000
United States	1000.000

Non allocated shares   1.250

Total   10,000.000

Source: EBRD/Annex A of the Agreement establishing the European Bank for Reconstruction and Development.

Appendix 3

Letter from the head of the Soviet delegation to the chairman of the constitutive conference regarding the access of the Soviet Union to EBRD resources

To the Chairman of the Conference
on the Establishment of the
European Bank for
Reconstruction and Development

M. Chairman,

As you know, the initiative of the President of France M. P. Mitterrand to establish the European Bank for Reconstruction and Development for the purpose of facilitating the transition of Central and Eastern European countries towards market-oriented economies has found understanding and support on behalf of the Soviet authorities. The Soviet delegation participated in the sessions of talks on drafting the constituent documents of the Bank. As a result the constituent countries have reached considerable progress in drawing up the Agreement establishing the European Bank for Reconstruction and Development.

At the same time, certain difficulties largely stem from fears of a number of countries that due to the size of its economy the Soviet Union may become the principal recipient of credits of the Bank and therefore will narrow its capacity to extend aid to other Central and Eastern European Countries.

In this connexion I would like to assure you, dear Mr. Chairman, that the intentions of the Soviet Union to become an equal member of the Bank account primarily for its will to establish a new institution of multilateral co-operation so as to foster historical reforms on the European continent.

I would like to inform you that my government is prepared to limit its access to the Bank's resources, pursuant to paragraph 4 of Article 8 of the Articles of Agreement of the Bank, for a period of three years starting from the entry into force of the Articles of Agreement of the Bank.

During that period, the Soviet Union wishes that the Bank will provide technical assistance and other types of assistance directed to finance its private sector, to facilitate the transition of state-owned enterprises to private sector ownership and control and to help enterprises operating competitively and moving to participation in the market-oriented economy, subject to the proportion set forth in paragraph 3 of Article 11 of this Agreement. The total amount of any assistance thus provided by the Bank would not exceed the total amount of the cash disbursed and the promissory notes issued by the Soviet Union for its shares.

I am confident, that continuing economic reforms in the Soviet Union will inevitably promote the expansion of the Bank's activities into the territory of the Soviet Union. However, the USSR, being interested in securing the multilateral character of the Bank, will not choose that at any time in future the Soviet borrowings will exceed an amount consistent with maintaining the necessary diversity in the bank's operations and prudent limits on its exposure.

Please accept, Mr. Chairman, the assurances of my highest consideration.

Head of Soviet Delegation
Chairman of the Board
of the State Bank of the USSR
Victor V. Gerashchenko

Source: EBRD/Agreement establishing the European Bank for Reconstruction and Development.

Appendix 4

Agreement establishing the European Bank for Reconstruction and Development; Preamble and Articles

The Contracting Parties,

Committed to the fundamental principles of multiparty democracy, the rule of law, respect for human rights and market economics;

Recalling the Final Act of the Helsinki Conference on Security and Cooperation in Europe, and in particular its Declaration on Principles;

Welcoming the intent of Central and Eastern European countries to further the practical implementation of multiparty democracy, strengthening democratic institutions, the rule of law and respect for human rights and their willingness to implement reforms in order to evolve towards market-oriented economies;

Considering the importance of close and coordinated cooperation in order to promote the economic progress of Central and Eastern European countries to help their economies become more internationally competitive and assist them in their reconstruction and development and thus to reduce, where appropriate, any risks related to the financing of their economies;

Convinced that the establishment of a multilateral financial institution which is European in its basic character and broadly international in its membership would help serve these ends and would constitute a new and unique structure of cooperation in Europe;

Have agreed to establish hereby the European Bank for Reconstruction and Development (hereinafter called "the Bank") which shall operate in accordance with the following:

Chapter I

PURPOSE, FUNCTIONS AND MEMBERSHIP

Article 1

PURPOSE

In contributing to economic progress and reconstruction, the purpose of the Bank shall be to foster the transition towards open market-oriented economies and to promote private and entrepreneurial initiative in the Central and Eastern European countries committed to and applying the principles of multiparty democracy, pluralism and market economics.

Article 2

FUNCTIONS

1. To fulfil on a long-term basis its purpose of fostering the transition of Central and Eastern European countries towards open market-oriented economies and the promotion of private and entrepreneurial initiative, the Bank shall assist the recipient member countries to implement structural and sectoral economic reforms, including demonopolization, decentralization and privatization, to help their economies become fully integrated into the international economy by measures:

(i) to promote, through private and other interested investors, the establishment, improvement and expansion of productive, competitive and private sector activity, in particular small and medium sized enterprises;

(ii) to mobilize domestic and foreign capital and experienced management to the end described in (i);

(iii) to foster productive investment, including in the service and financial sectors, and in related infrastructure where that is necessary to support private and entrepreneurial initiative, thereby assisting in making a competitive environment and raising productivity, the standard of living and conditions of labour;

(iv) to provide technical assistance for the preparation, financing and implementation of relevant projects, whether individual or in the context of specific investment programmes;

(v) to stimulate and encourage the development of capital markets;

(vi) to give support to sound and economically viable projects involving more than one recipient member country;

(vii) to promote in the full range of its activities environmentally sound and sustainable development; and

(viii) to undertake such other activities and provide such other services as may further these functions.

2. In carrying out the functions referred to in paragraph 1 of this Article, the Bank shall work in close cooperation with all its members and, in such manner as it may deem appropriate within the terms of this Agreement, with the International Monetary Fund, the International Bank for Reconstruction and Development, the International Finance Corporation, the Multilateral Investment Guarantee Agency, and the Organization for Economic Cooperation and Development, and shall cooperate with the United Nations and its Specialised Agencies and other related bodies, and any entity, whether public or private, concerned with the economic development of, and investment in, Central and Eastern European countries.

Article 3

MEMBERSHIP

1. Membership in the Bank shall be open:

    (i)   to (1) European countries and (2) non-European countries which are members of the International Monetary Fund; and
    (ii) to the European Economic Community and the European Investment Bank.

2. Countries eligible for membership under paragraph 1 of this Article, which do not become members in accordance with Article 61 of this Agreement, may be admitted, under such terms and conditions as the Bank may determine, to membership in the Bank upon the affirmative vote of not less than two-thirds of the Governors, representing not less than three-fourths of the total voting power of the members.

Chapter II

CAPITAL

Article 4

AUTHORIZED CAPITAL STOCK

1. The original authorized capital stock shall be ten thousand million (10,000,000,000) ECU. It shall be divided into one million (1,000,000) shares, having a par value of ten thousand (10,000) ECU each, which shall be available for subscription only by members in accordance with the provisions of Article 5 of this Agreement.

2. The original capital stock shall be divided into paid-in shares and callable shares. The initial total aggregate par value of paid-in shares shall be three thousand million (3,000,000,000) ECU.

3. The authorized capital stock may be increased at such time and under such terms as may seem advisable, by a vote of not less

than two-thirds of the Governors, representing not less than three-fourths of the total voting power of the members.

Article 5

SUBSCRIPTION OF SHARES

1.   Each member shall subscribe to shares of the capital stock of the Bank, subject to fulfilment of the member's legal requirements. Each subscription to the original authorized capital stock shall be for paid-in shares and callable shares in the proportion of three (3) to seven (7). The initial number of shares available to be subscribed to by Signatories to this Agreement which become members in accordance with Article 61 of this Agreement shall be that set forth in Annex A. No member shall have an initial subscription of less than one hundred (100) shares.

2.   The initial number of shares to be subscribed to by countries which are admitted to membership in accordance with paragraph 2 of Article 3 of this Agreement shall be determined by the Board of Governors; provided, however, that no such subscription shall be authorized which would have the effect of reducing the percentage of capital stock held by countries which are members of the European Economic Community, together with the European Economic Community and the European Investment Bank, below the majority of the total subscribed capital stock.

3.   The Board of Governors shall at intervals of not more than five (5) years review the capital stock of the Bank. In case of an increase in the authorized capital stock, each member shall have a reasonable opportunity to subscribe, under such uniform terms and conditions as the Board of Governors shall determine, to a proportion of the increase in stock equivalent to the proportion which its stock subscribed bears to the total subscribed capital stock immediately prior to such increase. No member shall be obliged to subscribe to any part of an increase of capital stock.

4.   Subject to the provisions of paragraph 3 of this Article, the Board of Governors may, at the request of a member, increase the subscription of that member, or allocate shares to that member within the authorized capital stock which are not taken up by other members; provided, however, that such increase shall not

have the effect of reducing the percentage of capital stock held by countries which are members of the European Economic Community, together with the European Economic Community and the European Investment Bank, below the majority of the total subscribed capital stock.

5.   Shares of stock initially subscribed to by members shall be issued at par. Other shares shall be issued at par unless the Board of Governors, by a vote of not less than two-thirds of the Governors, representing not less than two-thirds of the total voting power of the members, decides to issue them in special circumstances on other terms.

6.   Shares of stock shall not be pledged or encumbered in any manner whatsoever, and they shall not be transferable except to the Bank in accordance with Chapter VII of this Agreement.

7.   The liability of the members on shares shall be limited to the unpaid portion of their issue price. No member shall be liable, by reason of its membership, for obligations of the Bank.

Article 6

PAYMENT OF SUBSCRIPTIONS

1.   Payment of the paid-in shares of the amount initially subscribed to by each Signatory to this Agreement, which becomes a member in accordance with Article 61 of this Agreement, shall be made in five (5) instalments of twenty (20) per cent each of such amount. The first instalment shall be paid by each member within sixty (60) days after the date of the entry into force of this Agreement, or after the date of deposit of its instrument of ratification, acceptance or approval in accordance with Article 61, if this latter is later than the date of the entry into force. The remaining four (4) instalments shall each become due successively one year from the date on which the preceding instalment became due and shall each, subject to the legislative requirements of each member, be paid.

2.   Fifty (50) per cent of payment of each instalment pursuant to paragraph 1 of this Article, or by a member admitted in accordance with paragraph 2 of Article 3 of this Agreement, may be made in promissory notes or other obligations issued by such member and denominated in ECU, in United States dollars or in

Japanese yen, to be drawn down as the Bank needs funds for disbursement as a result of its operations. Such notes or obligations shall be non-negotiable, non-interest-bearing and payable to the Bank at par value upon demand. Demands upon such notes or obligations shall, over reasonable periods of time, be made so that the value of such demands in ECU at the time of demand from each member is proportional to the number of paid-in shares subscribed to and held by each such member depositing such notes or obligations.

3. All payment obligations of a member in respect of subscription to shares in the initial capital stock shall be settled either in ECU, in United States dollars or in Japanese yen on the basis of the average exchange rate of the relevant currency in terms of the ECU for the period from 30 September 1989 to 31 March 1990 inclusive.

4. Payment of the amount subscribed to the callable capital stock of the Bank shall be subject to call, taking account of Articles 17 and 42 of this Agreement, only as and when required by the Bank to meet its liabilities.

5. In the event of a call referred to in paragraph 4 of this Article, payment shall be made by the member in ECU, in United States dollars or in Japanese yen. Such calls shall be uniform in ECU value upon each callable share calculated at the time of the call.

6. The Bank shall determine the place for any payment under this Article not later than one month after the inaugural meeting of its Board of Governors, provided that, before such determination, the payment of the first instalment referred to in paragraph 1 of this Article shall be made to the European Investment Bank, as trustee for the Bank.

7. For subscriptions other than those described in paragraphs 1, 2 and 3 of this Article, payments by a member in respect of subscription to paid-in shares in the authorized capital stock shall be made in ECU, in United States dollars or in Japanese yen whether in cash or in promissory notes or in other obligations.

8. For the purposes of this Article, payment or denomination in ECU shall include payment or denomination in any fully convertible currency which is equivalent on the date of payment or encashment to the value of the relevant obligation in ECU.

Article 7

ORDINARY CAPITAL RESOURCES

As used in this Agreement, the term "ordinary capital resources" of the Bank shall include the following:

(i)   authorized capital stock of the Bank, including both paid-in and callable shares, subscribed to pursuant to Article 5 of this Agreement;

(ii)   funds raised by borrowings of the Bank by virtue of powers conferred by sub-paragraph (i) of Article 20 of this Agreement, to which the commitment to calls provided for in paragraph 4 of Article 6 of this Agreement is applicable;

(iii)   funds received in repayment of loans or guarantees and proceeds from the disposal of equity investment made with the resources indicated in sub-paragraphs (i) and (ii) of this Article;

(iv)   income derived from loans and equity investment, made from the resources indicated in sub-paragraphs (i) and (ii) of this Article, and income derived from guarantees and underwriting not forming part of the special operations of the Bank; and

(v)   any other funds or income received by the Bank which do not form part of its Special Funds resources referred to in Article 19 of this Agreement.

Chapter III

OPERATIONS

Article 8

RECIPIENT COUNTRIES AND USE OF RESOURCES

1. The resources and facilities of the Bank shall be used exclusively to implement the purpose and carry out the functions set forth, respectively, in Articles 1 and 2 of this Agreement.

2. The Bank may conduct its operations in countries from Central and Eastern Europe which are proceeding steadily in the transition towards market-oriented economies and the promotion of private and entrepreneurial initiative, and which apply, by concrete steps and otherwise, the principles as set forth in Article 1 of this Agreement.

3. In cases where a member might be implementing policies which are inconsistent with Article 1 of this Agreement, or in exceptional circumstances, the Board of Directors shall consider whether access by a member to Bank resources should be suspended or otherwise modified and may make recommendations accordingly to the Board of Governors. Any decision on these matters shall be taken by the Board of Governors by a majority of not less than two-thirds of the Governors, representing not less than three-fourths of the total voting power of the members.

4.   (i)   Any potential recipient country may request that the Bank provide access to its resources for limited purposes over a period of three (3) years beginning after the entry into force of this Agreement. Any such request shall be attached as an integral part of this Agreement as soon as it is made.

      (ii)   During such a period:

         (a)   the Bank shall provide to such a country, and to enterprises in its territory, upon their request, technical assistance and other types of assistance directed to finance its private sector, to facilitate the transition of state-owned enterprises to private ownership and control, and to help enterprises operating competitively and moving to participation in the market oriented economy, subject to the proportion set forth in paragraph 3 of Article 11 of this Agreement;

         (b)   the total amount of any assistance thus provided shall not exceed the total amount of cash disbursed and promissory notes issued by that country for its shares.

(iii)   At the end of this period, the decision to allow such a country access beyond the limits specified in sub-paragraphs (a) and (b) shall be taken by the Board of Governors by a majority of not less than three-fourths of the Governors representing not less than eighty-five (85) per cent of the total voting power of the members.

Article 9

ORDINARY AND SPECIAL OPERATIONS

The operations of the Bank shall consist of ordinary operations financed from the ordinary capital resources of the Bank referred to in Article 7 of this Agreement and special operations financed from the Special Funds resources referred to in Article 19 of this Agreement. The two types of operations may be combined.

Article 10

SEPARATION OF OPERATIONS

1.   The ordinary capital resources and the Special Funds resources of the Bank shall at all times and in all respects be held, used, committed, invested or otherwise disposed of entirely separately from each other. The financial statements of the Bank shall show the reserves of the Bank, together with its ordinary operations, and, separately, its special operations.

2.   The ordinary capital resources of the Bank shall under no circumstances be charged with, or used to discharge, losses or liabilities arising out of special operations or other activities for which Special Funds resources were originally used or committed.

3.   Expenses appertaining directly to ordinary operations shall be charged to the ordinary capital resources of the Bank. Expenses appertaining directly to special operations shall be charged to Special Funds resources. Any other expenses shall, subject to paragraph 1 of Article 18 of this Agreement, be charged as the Bank shall determine.

Article 11

METHODS OF OPERATION

1. The Bank shall carry out its operations in furtherance of its purpose and functions as set out in Articles 1 and 2 of this Agreement in any or all of the following ways:

   (i)   by making, or cofinancing together with multilateral institutions, commercial banks or other interested sources, or participating in, loans to private sector enterprises, loans to any state-owned enterprise operating competitively and moving to participation in the market-oriented economy, and loans to any state-owned enterprise to facilitate its transition to private ownership and control; in particular to facilitate or enhance the participation of private and/or foreign capital in such enterprises;

   (ii) (a) by investment in the equity capital of private sector enterprises;

          (b) by investment in the equity capital of any state-owned enterprise operating competitively and moving to participation in the market-oriented economy, and investment in the equity capital of any state-owned enterprise to facilitate its transition to private ownership and control; in particular to facilitate or enhance the participation of private and/or foreign capital in such enterprises; and

          (c) by underwriting, where other means of financing are not appropriate, the equity issue of securities by both private sector enterprises and such state-owned enterprises referred to in (b) above for the ends mentioned in that sub-paragraph;

   (iii) by facilitating access to domestic and international capital markets by private sector enterprises or by other enterprises referred to in subparagraph (i) of this paragraph for the ends mentioned in that sub-paragraph, through the provision of guarantees, where other means of financing are not appropriate, and through financial advice and other forms of assistance;

(iv)   by deploying Special Funds resources in accordance with the agreements determining their use; and

(v)   by making or participating in loans and providing technical assistance for the reconstruction or development of infrastructure, including environmental programmes, necessary for private sector development and the transition to a market-oriented economy.

For the purposes of this paragraph, a state-owned enterprise shall not be regarded as operating competitively unless it operates autonomously in a competitive market environment and unless it is subject to bankruptcy laws.

2.   (i)   The Board of Directors shall review at least annually the Bank's operations and lending strategy in each recipient country to ensure that the purpose and the functions of the Bank, as set out in Articles 1 and 2 of this Agreement, are fully served. Any decision pursuant to such a review shall be taken by a majority of not less than two-thirds of the Directors, representing not less than three-fourths of the total voting power of the members.

(ii)   The said review shall involve the consideration of, *inter alia*, each recipient country's progress made on decentralization, demonopolization and privatization and the relative shares of the Bank's lending to private enterprises, to state-owned enterprises in the process of transition to participation in the market-oriented economy or privatization, for infrastructure, for technical assistance, and for other purposes.

3.   (i)   Not more than forty (40) per cent of the amount of the Bank's total committed loans, guarantees and equity investments, without prejudice to its other operations referred to in this Article, shall be provided to the state sector. Such percentage limit shall apply initially over a two (2) year period, from the date of commencement of the Bank's operations,

taking one year with another, and thereafter in respect of each subsequent financial year.

(ii) For any country, not more than forty (40) per cent of the amount of the Bank's total committed loans, guarantees and equity investments over a period of five (5) years, taking one year with another, and without prejudice to the Bank's other operations referred to in this Article, shall be provided to the state sector.

(iii) For the purposes of this paragraph,

(a) the state sector includes national and local governments, their agencies, and enterprises owned or controlled by any of them;

(b) a loan or guarantee to, or equity investment in, a state-owned enterprise which is implementing a programme to achieve private ownership and control shall not be considered as made to the state sector;

(c) loans to a financial intermediary for onlending to the private sector shall not be considered as made to the state sector.

Article 12

LIMITATIONS ON ORDINARY OPERATIONS

1. The total amount of outstanding loans, equity investments and guarantees made by the Bank in its ordinary operations shall not be increased at any time, if by such increase the total amount of its unimpaired subscribed capital, reserves and surpluses included in its ordinary capital resources would be exceeded.

2. The amount of any equity investment shall not normally exceed such percentage of the equity capital of the enterprise concerned as shall be determined, by a general rule, to be appropriate by the Board of Directors. The Bank shall not seek to obtain by such an investment a controlling interest in the enterprise concerned and shall not exercise such control or assume direct responsibility for managing any enterprise in which it has an investment, except in the event of actual or threatened default on any of its investments, actual or threatened insolvency

of the enterprise in which such investment shall have been made, or other situations which, in the opinion of the Bank, threaten to jeopardize such investment, in which case the Bank may take such action and exercise such rights as it may deem necessary for the protection of its interests.

3.   The amount of the Bank's disbursed equity investments shall not at any time exceed an amount corresponding to its total unimpaired paid-in subscribed capital, surpluses and general reserve.

4.   The Bank shall not issue guarantees for export credits nor undertake insurance activities.

Article 13

OPERATING PRINCIPLES

The Bank shall operate in accordance with the following principles:

(i)   the Bank shall apply sound banking principles to all its operations;

(ii)   the operations of the Bank shall provide for the financing of specific projects, whether individual or in the context of specific investment programmes, and for technical assistance, designed to fulfil its purpose and functions as set out in Articles 1 and 2 of this Agreement;

(iii)   the Bank shall not finance any undertaking in the territory of a member if that member objects to such financing;

(iv)   the Bank shall not allow a disproportionate amount of its resources to be used for the benefit of any member;

(v)   the Bank shall seek to maintain reasonable diversification in all its investments;

(vi)   before a loan, guarantee or equity investment is granted, the applicant shall have submitted an adequate proposal and the President of the Bank shall have presented to the Board of Directors a written report regarding the proposal, together with recommendations, on the basis of a staff study;

(vii) the Bank shall not undertake any financing, or provide any facilities, when the applicant is able to obtain sufficient financing or facilities elsewhere on terms and conditions that the Bank considers reasonable;

(viii) in providing or guaranteeing financing, the Bank shall pay due regard to the prospect that the borrower and its guarantor, if any, will be in a position to meet their obligations under the financing contract;

(ix) in case of a direct loan made by the Bank, the borrower shall be permitted by the Bank to draw its funds only to meet expenditure as it is actually incurred;

(x) the Bank shall seek to revolve its funds by selling its investments to private investors whenever it can appropriately do so on satisfactory terms;

(xi) in its investments in individual enterprises, the Bank shall undertake its financing on terms and conditions which it considers appropriate, taking into account the requirements of the enterprise, the risks being undertaken by the Bank, and the terms and conditions normally obtained by private investors for similar financing;

(xii) the Bank shall place no restriction upon the procurement of goods and services from any country from the proceeds of any loan, investment or other financing undertaking in the ordinary or special operations of the Bank, and shall, in all appropriate cases, make its loans and other operations conditional on international invitations to tender being arranged; and

(xiii) the Bank shall take the necessary measures to ensure that the proceeds of any loan made, guaranteed or participated in by the Bank, or any equity investment, are used only for the purposes for which the loan or the equity investment was granted and with due attention to considerations of economy and efficiency.

Article 14

TERMS AND CONDITIONS FOR LOANS AND GUARANTEES

1. In the case of loans made, participated in, or guaranteed by the Bank, the contract shall establish the terms and conditions for the loan or the guarantee concerned, including those relating to payment of principal, interest and other fees, charges, maturities and dates of payment in respect of the loan or the guarantee, respectively. In setting such terms and conditions, the Bank shall take fully into account the need to safeguard its income.

2. Where the recipient of loans or guarantees of loans is not itself a member, but is a state-owned enterprise, the Bank may, when it appears desirable, bearing in mind the different approaches appropriate to public and state-owned enterprises in transition to private ownership and control, require the member or members in whose territory the project concerned is to be carried out, or a public agency or any instrumentality of such member or members acceptable to the Bank, to guarantee the repayment of the principal and the payment of interest and other fees and charges of the loan in accordance with the terms thereof. The Board of Directors shall review annually the Bank's practice in this matter, paying due attention to the Bank's creditworthiness.

3. The loan or guarantee contract shall expressly state the currency or currencies, or ECU, in which all payments to the Bank thereunder shall be made.

Article 15

COMMISSION AND FEES

1. The Bank shall charge, in addition to interest, a commission on loans made or participated in as part of its ordinary operations. The terms and conditions of this commission shall be determined by the Board of Directors.

2. In guaranteeing a loan as part of its ordinary operations, or in underwriting the sale of securities, the Bank shall charge fees, payable at rates and times determined by the Board of Directors, to provide suitable compensation for its risks.

3. The Board of Directors may determine any other charges

of the Bank in its ordinary operations and any commission, fees or other charges in its special operations.

Article 16

SPECIAL RESERVE

1. The amount of commissions and fees received by the Bank pursuant to Article 15 of this Agreement shall be set aside as a special reserve which shall be kept for meeting the losses of the Bank in accordance with Article 17 of this Agreement. The special reserve shall be held in such liquid form as the Bank may decide.

2. If the Board of Directors determines that the size of the special reserve is adequate, it may decide that all or part of the said commission or fees shall henceforth form part of the income of the Bank.

Article 17

METHODS OF MEETING THE LOSSES OF THE BANK

1. In the Bank's ordinary operations, in cases of arrears or default on loans made, participated in, or guaranteed by the Bank, and in cases of losses on underwriting and in equity investment, the Bank shall take such action as it deems appropriate. The Bank shall maintain appropriate provisions against possible losses.

2. Losses arising in the Bank's ordinary operations shall be charged:

   (i)   first, to the provisions referred to in paragraph 1 of this Article;
   (ii)   second, to net income;
   (iii) third, against the special reserve provided for in Article 16 of this Agreement;
   (iv)   fourth, against its general reserve and surpluses;
   (v)   fifth, against the unimpaired paid-in capital; and
   (vi)   last, against an appropriate amount of the uncalled subscribed callable capital which shall be called in accordance with the provisions of paragraphs 4 and 5 of Article 6 of this Agreement.

Article 18

SPECIAL FUNDS

1. The Bank may accept the administration of Special Funds which are designed to serve the purpose and come within the functions of the Bank. The full cost of administering any such Special Fund shall be charged to that Special Fund.

2. Special Funds accepted by the Bank may be used in any manner and on any terms and conditions consistent with the purpose and the functions of the Bank, with the other applicable provisions of this Agreement, and with the agreement or agreements relating to such Funds.

3. The Bank shall adopt such rules and regulations as may be required for the establishment, administration and use of each Special Fund. Such rules and regulations shall be consistent with the provisions of this Agreement, except for those provisions expressly applicable only to ordinary operations of the Bank.

Article 19

SPECIAL FUNDS RESOURCES

The term "Special Funds resources" shall refer to the resources of any Special Fund and shall include:

(i)   funds accepted by the Bank for inclusion in any Special Fund;

(ii) funds repaid in respect of loans or guarantees, and the proceeds of equity investments, financed from the resources of any Special Fund which, under the rules and regulations governing that Special Fund, are received by such Special Fund; and

(iii) income derived from investment of Special Funds resources.

Chapter IV

BORROWING AND OTHER MISCELLANEOUS POWERS

Article 20

GENERAL POWERS

1. The Bank shall have, in addition to the powers specified elsewhere in this Agreement, the power to:

(i)   borrow funds in member countries or elsewhere, provided always that:
  (a)   before making a sale of its obligations in the territory of a country, the Bank shall have obtained its approval; and
  (b)   where the obligations of the Bank are to be denominated in the currency of a member, the Bank shall have obtained its approval;

(ii)   invest or deposit funds not needed in its operations;

(iii)   buy and sell securities, in the secondary market, which the Bank has issued or guaranteed or in which it has invested;

(iv)   guarantee securities in which it has invested in order to facilitate their sale;

(v)   underwrite, or participate in the underwriting of, securities issued by any enterprise for purposes consistent with the purpose and functions of the Bank;

(vi)   provide technical advice and assistance which serve its purpose and come within its functions;

(vii)   exercise such other powers and adopt such rules and regulations as may be necessary or appropriate in furtherance of its purpose and functions, consistent with the provisions of this Agreement; and

(viii)   conclude agreements of cooperation with any public or private entity or entities.

2. Every security issued or guaranteed by the Bank shall bear on its face a conspicuous statement to the effect that it is not an

obligation of any Government or member, unless it is in fact the obligation of a particular Government or member, in which case it shall so state.

Chapter V

CURRENCIES

Article 21

DETERMINATION AND USE OF CURRENCIES

1.   Whenever it shall become necessary under this Agreement to determine whether any currency is fully convertible for the purposes of this Agreement, such determination shall be made by the Bank, taking into account the paramount need to preserve its own financial interests, after consultation, if necessary, with the International Monetary Fund.

2.   Members shall not impose any restrictions on the receipt, holding, use or transfer by the Bank of the following:

   (i)   currencies or ECU received by the Bank in payment of subscriptions to its capital stock, in accordance with Article 6 of this Agreement;
   (ii)   currencies obtained by the Bank by borrowing;
   (iii) currencies and other resources administered by the Bank as contributions to Special Funds; and
   (iv)   currencies received by the Bank in payment on account of principal, interest, dividends or other charges in respect of loans or investments, or the proceeds of disposal of such investments made out of any of the funds referred to in sub-paragraphs (i) to (iii) of this paragraph, or in payment of commission, fees or other charges.

Chapter VI

ORGANIZATION AND MANAGEMENT

Article 22

STRUCTURE

The Bank shall have a Board of Governors, a Board of Directors, a President, one or more Vice-Presidents and such other officers and staff as may be considered necessary.

Article 23

BOARD OF GOVERNORS: COMPOSITION

1. Each member shall be represented on the Board of Governors and shall appoint one Governor and one Alternate. Each Governor and Alternate shall serve at the pleasure of the appointing member. No Alternate may vote except in the absence of his or her principal. At each of its annual meetings, the Board shall elect one of the Governors as Chairman who shall hold office until the election of the next Chairman.

2. Governors and Alternates shall serve as such without remuneration from the Bank.

Article 24

BOARD OF GOVERNORS: POWERS

1. All the powers of the Bank shall be vested in the Board of Governors.

2. The Board of Governors may delegate to the Board of Directors any or all of its powers, except the power to:

  (i)   admit new members and determine the conditions of their admission;
  (ii)   increase or decrease the authorized capital stock of the Bank;
  (iii) suspend a member;

(iv) decide appeals from interpretations or applications of this Agreement given by the Board of Directors;

(v) authorize the conclusion of general agreements for co-operation with other international organizations;

(vi) elect the Directors and the President of the Bank;

(vii) determine the remuneration of the Directors and Alternate Directors and the salary and other terms of the contract of service of the President;

(viii) approve, after reviewing the auditors' report, the general balance sheet and the statement of profit and loss of the Bank;

(ix) determine the reserves and the allocation and distribution of the net profits of the Bank;

(x) amend this Agreement;

(xi) decide to terminate the operations of the Bank and to distribute its assets; and

(xii) exercise such other powers as are expressly assigned to the Board of Governors in this Agreement.

3. The Board of Governors shall retain full power to exercise authority over any matter delegated or assigned to the Board of Directors under paragraph 2 of this Article, or elsewhere in this Agreement.

Article 25

BOARD OF GOVERNORS: PROCEDURE

1. The Board of Governors shall hold an annual meeting and such other meetings as may be provided for by the Board or called by the Board of Directors. Meetings of the Board of Governors shall be called, by the Board of Directors, whenever requested by not less than five (5) members of the Bank or members holding not less than one quarter of the total voting power of the members.

2. Two-thirds of the Governors shall constitute a quorum for any meeting of the Board of Governors, provided such majority represents not less than two-thirds of the total voting power of the members.

3. The Board of Governors may by regulation establish a procedure whereby the Board of Directors may, when the latter

deems such action advisable, obtain a vote of the Governors on a specific question without calling a meeting of the Board of Governors.

4. The Board of Governors, and the Board of Directors to the extent authorized, may adopt such rules and regulations and establish such subsidiary bodies as may be necessary or appropriate to conduct the business of the Bank.

Article 26

BOARD OF DIRECTORS: COMPOSITION

1. The Board of Directors shall be composed of twenty-three (23) members who shall not be members of the Board of Governors, and of whom:

    (i)   Eleven (11) shall be elected by the Governors representing Belgium, Denmark, France, the Federal Republic of Germany, Greece, Ireland, Italy, Luxembourg, the Netherlands, Portugal, Spain, the United Kingdom, the European Economic Community and the European Investment Bank; and

    (ii)   Twelve (12) shall be elected by the Governors representing other members, of whom:

        (a)   four (4), by the Governors representing those countries listed in Annex A as Central and Eastern European countries eligible for assistance from the Bank;

        (b)   four (4), by the Governors representing those countries listed in Annex A as other European countries;

        (c)   four (4), by the Governors representing those countries listed in Annex A as non-European countries.

Directors, as well as representing members whose Governors have elected them, may also represent members who assign their votes to them.

2. Directors shall be persons of high competence in economic and financial matters and shall be elected in accordance with Annex B.

3. The Board of Governors may increase or decrease the size, or revise the composition, of the Board of Directors, in order to take into account changes in the number of members of the Bank, by an affirmative vote of not less than two-thirds of the Governors, representing not less than three-fourths of the total voting power of the members. Without prejudice to the exercise of these powers for subsequent elections, the number and composition of the second Board of Directors shall be as set out in paragraph 1 of this Article.

4. Each Director shall appoint an Alternate with full power to act for him or her when he or she is not present. Directors and Alternates shall be nationals of member countries. No member shall be represented by more than one Director. An Alternate may participate in meetings of the Board but may vote only when he or she is acting in place of his or her principal.

5. Directors shall hold office for a term of three (3) years and may be reelected; provided that the first Board of Directors shall be elected by the Board of Governors at its inaugural meeting, and shall hold office until the next immediately following annual meeting of the Board of Governors or, if that Board shall so decide at that annual meeting, until its next subsequent annual meeting. They shall continue in office until their successors shall have been chosen and assumed office. If the office of a Director becomes vacant more than one hundred and eighty (180) days before the end of his or her term, a successor shall be chosen in accordance with Annex B, for the remainder of the term, by the Governors who elected the former Director. A majority of the votes cast by such Governors shall be required for such election. If the office of a Director becomes vacant one hundred and eighty (180) days or less before the end of his or her term, a successor may similarly be chosen for the remainder of the term, by the votes cast by such Governors who elected the former Director, in which election a majority of the votes cast by such Governors shall be required. While the office remains vacant, the Alternate of the former Director shall exercise the powers of the latter, except that of appointing an Alternate.

Article 27

BOARD OF DIRECTORS: POWERS

Without prejudice to the powers of the Board of Governors as provided in Article 24 of this Agreement, the Board of Directors shall be responsible for the direction of the general operations of the Bank and, for this purpose, shall, in addition to the powers assigned to it expressly by this Agreement, exercise all the powers delegated to it by the Board of Governors, and in particular:

(i)   prepare the work of the Board of Governors;

(ii)   in conformity with the general directions of the Board of Governors, establish policies and take decisions concerning loans, guarantees, investments in equity capital, borrowing by the Bank, the furnishing of technical assistance, and other operations of the Bank;

(iii) submit the audited accounts for each financial year for approval of the Board of Governors at each annual meeting; and

(iv) approve the budget of the Bank.

Article 28

BOARD OF DIRECTORS: PROCEDURE

1. The Board of Directors shall normally function at the principal office of the Bank and shall meet as often as the business of the Bank may require.

2. A majority of the Directors shall constitute a quorum for any meeting of the Board of Directors, provided such majority represents not less than two-thirds of the total voting power of the members.

3. The Board of Governors shall adopt regulations under which, if there is no Director of its nationality, a member may send a representative to attend, without right to vote, any meeting of the Board of Directors when a matter particularly affecting that member is under consideration.

Article 29

VOTING

1.   The voting power of each member shall be equal to the number of its subscribed shares in the capital stock of the Bank. In the event of any member failing to pay any part of the amount due in respect of its obligations in relation to paid-in shares under Article 6 of this Agreement, such member shall be unable for so long as such failure continues to exercise that percentage of its voting power which corresponds to the percentage which the amount due but unpaid bears to the total amount of paid-in shares subscribed to by that member in the capital stock of the Bank.

2.   In voting in the Board of Governors, each Governor shall be entitled to cast the votes of the member he or she represents. Except as otherwise expressly provided in this Agreement, all matters before the Board of Governors shall be decided by a majority of the voting power of the members voting.

3.   In voting in the Board of Directors each Director shall be entitled to cast the number of votes to which the Governors who have elected him or her are entitled and those to which any Governors who have assigned their votes to him or her, pursuant to Section D of Annex B, are entitled. A Director representing more than one member may cast separately the votes of the members he or she represents. Except as otherwise expressly provided in this Agreement, and except for general policy decisions in which cases such policy decisions shall be taken by a majority of not less than two-thirds of the total voting power of the members voting, all matters before the Board of Directors shall be decided by a majority of the voting power of the members voting.

Article 30

THE PRESIDENT

1.   The Board of Governors, by a vote of a majority of the total number of Governors, representing not less than a majority of the total voting power of the members, shall elect a President of the

Bank. The President, while holding office, shall not be a Governor or a Director or an Alternate for either.

2.   The term of office of the President shall be four (4) years. He or she may be re-elected. He or she shall, however, cease to hold office when the Board of Governors so decides by an affirmative vote of not less than two-thirds of the Governors, representing not less than two-thirds of the total voting power of the members. If the office of the President for any reason becomes vacant, the Board of Governors, in accordance with the provisions of paragraph 1 of this Article, shall elect a successor for up to four (4) years.

3.   The President shall not vote, except that he or she may cast a deciding vote in case of an equal division. He or she may participate in meetings of the Board of Governors and shall chair the meetings of the Board of Directors.

4.   The President shall be the legal representative of the Bank.

5.   The President shall be chief of the staff of the Bank. He or she shall be responsible for the organization, appointment and dismissal of the officers and staff in accordance with regulations to be adopted by the Board of Directors. In appointing officers and staff, he or she shall, subject to the paramount importance of efficiency and technical competence, pay due regard to recruitment on a wide geographical basis among members of the Bank.

6.   The President shall conduct, under the direction of the Board of Directors, the current business of the Bank.

Article 31

VICE PRESIDENT (S)

1.   One or more Vice-Presidents shall be appointed by the Board of Directors on the recommendation of the President. A Vice-President shall hold office for such term, exercise such authority and perform such functions in the administration of the Bank, as may be determined by the Board of Directors. In the absence or incapacity of the President, a Vice-President shall exercise the authority and perform the functions of the President.

2.   A Vice-President may participate in meetings of the Board of Directors but shall have no vote at such meetings, except that

he or she may cast the deciding vote when acting in place of the President.

Article 32

INTERNATIONAL CHARACTER OF THE BANK

1.   The Bank shall not accept Special Funds or other loans or assistance that may in any way prejudice, deflect or otherwise alter its purpose or functions.

2.   The Bank, its President, Vice-President (s), officers and staff shall in their decisions take into account only considerations relevant to the Bank's purpose, functions and operations, as set out in this Agreement. Such considerations shall be weighed impartially in order to achieve and carry out the purpose and functions of the Bank.

3.   The President, Vice-President (s), officers and staff of the Bank, in the discharge of their offices, shall owe their duty entirely to the Bank and to no other authority. Each member of the Bank shall respect the international character of this duty and shall refrain from all attempts to influence any of them in the discharge of their duties.

Article 33

LOCATION OF OFFICES

1.   The principal office of the Bank shall be located in London.

2.   The Bank may establish agencies or branch offices in the territory of any member of the Bank.

Article 34

DEPOSITORIES AND CHANNELS OF COMMUNICATION

1.   Each member shall designate its central bank, or such other institution as may be agreed upon with the Bank, as a depository for all the Bank's holdings of its currency as well as other assets of the Bank.

2.   Each member shall designate an appropriate official entity with which the Bank may communicate in connection with any matter arising under this Agreement.

Article 35

PUBLICATION OF REPORTS AND PROVISION OF INFORMATION

1.   The Bank shall publish an annual report containing an audited statement of its accounts and shall circulate to members at intervals of three (3) months or less a summary statement of its financial position and a profit and loss statement showing the results of its operations. The financial accounts shall be kept in ECU.

2.   The Bank shall report annually on the environmental impact of its activities and may publish such other reports as it deems desirable to advance its purpose.

3.   Copies of all reports, statements and publications made under this Article shall be distributed to members.

Article 36

ALLOCATION AND DISTRIBUTION OF NET INCOME

1.   The Board of Governors shall determine at least annually what part of the Bank's net income, after making provision for reserves and, if necessary, against possible losses under paragraph 1 of Article 17 of this Agreement, shall be allocated to surplus or other purposes and what part, if any, shall be distributed. Any such decision on the allocation of the Bank's net income to other purposes shall be taken by a majority of not less than two-thirds of the Governors, representing not less than two-thirds of the total voting power of the members. No such allocation, and no distribution, shall be made until the general reserve amounts to at least ten (10) per cent of the authorized capital stock.

2.   Any distribution referred to in the preceding paragraph shall be made in proportion to the number of paid-in shares held by each member; provided that in calculating such number ac-

count shall be taken only of payments received in cash and promissory notes encashed in respect of such shares on or before the end of the relevant financial year.

3.   Payments to each member shall be made in such manner as the Board of Governors shall determine. Such payments and their use by the receiving country shall be without restriction by any member.

Chapter VII

WITHDRAWAL AND SUSPENSION OF MEMBERSHIP: TEMPORARY SUSPENSION AND TERMINATION OF OPERATIONS

Article 37

RIGHT OF MEMBERS TO WITHDRAW

1.   Any member may withdraw from the Bank at any time by transmitting a notice in writing to the Bank at its principal office.

2.   Withdrawal by a member shall become effective, and its membership shall cease, on the date specified in its notice but in no event less than six (6) months after such notice is received by the Bank. However, at any time before the withdrawal becomes finally effective, the member may notify the Bank in writing of the cancellation of its notice of intention to withdraw.

Article 38

SUSPENSION OF MEMBERSHIP

1.   If a member fails to fulfil any of its obligations to the Bank, the Bank may suspend its membership by decision of a majority of not less than two-thirds of the Governors, representing not less than two-thirds of the total voting power of the members. The member so suspended shall automatically cease to be a member one year from the date of its suspension unless a decision is taken by not less than the same majority to restore the member to good standing.

2.   While under suspension, a member shall not be entitled to exercise any rights under this Agreement, except the right of withdrawal, but shall remain subject to all its obligations.

Article 39

SETTLEMENT OF ACCOUNTS WITH FORMER MEMBERS

1.   After the date on which a member ceases to be a member, such former member shall remain liable for its direct obligations to the Bank and for its contingent liabilities to the Bank so long as any part of the loans, equity investments or guarantees contracted before it ceased to be a member are outstanding; but it shall cease to incur such liabilities with respect to loans, equity investments and guarantees entered into thereafter by the Bank and to share either in the income or the expenses of the Bank.

2.   At the time a member ceases to be a member, the Bank shall arrange for the repurchase of such former member's shares as a part of the settlement of accounts with such former member in accordance with the provisions of this Article. For this purpose, the repurchase price of the shares shall be the value shown by the books of the Bank on the date of cessation of membership, with the original purchase price of each share being its maximum value.

3.   The payment for shares repurchased by the Bank under this Article shall be governed by the following conditions:

(i)   any amount due to the former member for its shares shall be withheld so long as the former member, its central bank or any of its agencies or instrumentalities remains liable, as borrower or guarantor, to the Bank and such amount may, at the option of the Bank, be applied on any such liability as it matures. No amount shall be withheld on account of the liability of the former member resulting from its subscription for shares in accordance with paragraphs 4, 5 and 7 of Article 6 of this Agreement. In any event, no amount due to a member for its shares shall be paid until six (6) months after the date upon which the member ceases to be a member;

   (ii) payments for shares may be made from time to time, upon their surrender by the former member, to the extent by which the amount due as the repurchase price in accordance with paragraph 2 of this Article exceeds the aggregate amount of liabilities on loans, equity investments and guarantees in subparagraph (i) of this paragraph until the former member has received the full repurchase price;

 (iii) payments shall be made on such conditions and in such fully convertible currencies, or ECU, and on such dates, as the Bank determines; and

 (iv) if losses are sustained by the Bank on any guarantees, participations in loans, or loans which were outstanding on the date when the member ceased to be a member, or if a net loss is sustained by the Bank on equity investments held by it on such date, and the amount of such losses exceeds the amount of the reserves provided against losses on the date when the member ceased to be a member, such former member shall repay, upon demand, the amount by which the repurchase price of its shares would have been reduced if the losses had been taken into account when the repurchase price was determined. In addition, the former member shall remain liable on any call for unpaid subscriptions under paragraph 4 of Article 6 of this Agreement, to the extent that it would have been required to respond if the impairment of capital had occurred and the call had been made at the time the repurchase price of its shares was determined.

4.   If the Bank terminates its operations pursuant to Article 41 of this Agreement within six (6) months of the date upon which any member ceases to be a member, all rights of such former member shall be determined in accordance with the provisions of Articles 41 to 43 of this Agreement.

Article 40

TEMPORARY SUSPENSION OF OPERATIONS

In an emergency, the Board of Directors may suspend temporarily operations in respect of new loans, guarantees, underwriting, technical assistance and equity investments pending an opportunity for further consideration and action by the Board of Governors.

Article 41

TERMINATION OF OPERATIONS

The Bank may terminate its operations by the affirmative vote of not less than two-thirds of the Governors, representing not less than three-fourths of the total voting power of the members. Upon such termination of operations the Bank shall forthwith cease all activities, except those incident to the orderly realization, conservation and preservation of its assets and settlement of its obligations.

Article 42

LIABILITY OF MEMBERS AND PAYMENT OF CLAIMS

1.   In the event of termination of the operations of the Bank, the liability of all members for uncalled subscriptions to the capital stock of the Bank shall continue until all claims of creditors, including all contingent claims, shall have been discharged.

2.   Creditors on ordinary operations holding direct claims shall be paid first out of the assets of the Bank, secondly out of the payments to be made to the Bank in respect of unpaid paid-in shares, and then out of payments to be made to the Bank in respect of callable capital stock. Before making any payments to creditors holding direct claims, the Board of Directors shall make such arrangements as are necessary, in its judgment, to ensure a *pro rata* distribution among holders of direct and holders of contingent claims.

Article 43

DISTRIBUTION OF ASSETS

1.   No distribution under this Chapter shall be made to members on account of their subscriptions to the capital stock of the Bank until:

   (i)   all liabilities to creditors have been discharged or provided for; and
   (ii) the Board of Governors has decided by a vote of not less than two-thirds of the Governors, representing not less than three-fourths of the total voting power of the members, to make a distribution.

2.   Any distribution of the assets of the Bank to the members shall be in proportion to the capital stock held by each member and shall be effected at such times and under such conditions as the Bank shall deem fair and equitable.   The shares of assets distributed need not be uniform as to type of assets.   No member shall be entitled to receive its share in such a distribution of assets until it has settled all of its obligations to the Bank.

3.   Any member receiving assets distributed pursuant to this Article shall enjoy the same rights with respect to such assets as the Bank enjoyed prior to their distribution.

Chapter VIII

STATUS, IMMUNITIES, PRIVILEGES AND EXEMPTIONS

Article 44

PURPOSES OF CHAPTER

To enable the Bank to fulfil its purpose and the functions with which it is entrusted, the status, immunities, privileges and exemptions set forth in this Chapter shall be accorded to the Bank in the territory of each member country.

Article 45

STATUS OF THE BANK

The Bank shall possess full legal personality and, in particular, the full legal capacity:

(i)   to contract;
(ii)   to acquire, and dispose of, immovable and movable property; and
(iii) to institute legal proceedings.

Article 46

POSITION OF THE BANK WITH REGARD TO JUDICIAL PROCESS

Actions may be brought against the Bank only in a court of competent jurisdiction in the territory of a country in which the Bank has an office, has appointed an agent for the purpose of accepting service or notice of process, or has issued or guaranteed securities. No actions shall, however, be brought by members or persons acting for or deriving claims from members. The property and assets of the Bank shall, wheresoever located and by whomsoever held, be immune from all forms of seizure, attachment or execution before the delivery of final judgment against the Bank.

Article 47

IMMUNITY OF ASSETS FROM SEIZURE

Property and assets of the Bank, wheresoever located and by whomsoever held, shall be immune from search, requisition, confiscation, expropriation or any other form of taking or foreclosure by executive or legislative action.

Article 48

IMMUNITY OF ARCHIVES

The archives of the Bank, and in general all documents belonging to it or held by it, shall be inviolable.

Article 49

FREEDOM OF ASSETS FROM RESTRICTIONS

To the extent necessary to carry out the purpose and functions of the Bank and subject to the provisions of this Agreement, all property and assets of the Bank shall be free from restrictions, regulations, controls and moratoria of any nature.

Article 50

PRIVILEGE FOR COMMUNICATIONS

The official communications of the Bank shall be accorded by each member the same treatment that it accords to the official communications of any other member.

Article 51

IMMUNITIES OF OFFICERS AND EMPLOYEES

All Governors, Directors, Alternates, officers and employees of the Bank and experts performing missions for the Bank shall be immune from legal process with respect to acts performed by them in their official capacity, except when the Bank waives this immunity, and shall enjoy inviolability of all their official papers and documents. This immunity shall not apply, however, to civil liability in the case of damage arising from a road traffic accident caused by any such Governor, Director, Alternate, officer, employee or expert.

Article 52

PRIVILEGES OF OFFICERS AND EMPLOYEES

1. All Governors, Directors, Alternates, officers and employees of the Bank and experts of the Bank performing missions for the Bank:

     (i)   not being local nationals, shall be accorded the same immunities from immigration restrictions, alien registration requirements and national service obligations, and the same facilities as regards exchange regulations, as are accorded by members to the representatives, officials, and employees of comparable rank of other members; and

(ii) shall be granted the same treatment in respect of travelling facilities as is accorded by members to representatives, officials and employees of comparable rank of other members.

2.   The spouses and immediate dependents of those Directors, Alternate Directors, officers, employees and experts of the Bank who are resident in the country in which the principal office of the Bank is located shall be accorded opportunity to take employment in that country.   The spouses and immediate dependents of those Directors, Alternate Directors, officers, employees and experts of the Bank who are resident in a country in which any agency or branch office of the Bank is located should, wherever possible, in accordance with the national law of that country, be accorded similar opportunity in that country.   The Bank shall negotiate specific agreements implementing the provisions of this paragraph with the country in which the principal office of the Bank is located and, as appropriate, with the other countries concerned.

Article 53

EXEMPTION FROM TAXATION

1.   Within the scope of its official activities the Bank, its assets, property, and income shall be exempt from all direct taxes.

2.   When purchases or services of substantial value and necessary for the exercise of the official activities of the Bank are made or used by the Bank and when the price of such purchases or services includes taxes or duties, the member that has levied the taxes or duties shall, if they are identifiable, take appropriate measures to grant exemption from such taxes or duties or to provide for their reimbursement.

3.   Goods imported by the Bank and necessary for the exercise of its official activities shall be exempt from all import duties and

taxes, and from all import prohibitions and restrictions. Similarly goods exported by the Bank and necessary for the exercise of its official activities shall be exempt from all export duties and taxes, and from all export prohibitions and restrictions.

4. Goods acquired or imported and exempted under this Article shall not be sold, hired out, lent or given away against payment or free of charge, except in accordance with conditions laid down by the members which have granted exemptions or reimbursements.

5. The provisions of this Article shall not apply to taxes or duties which are no more than charges for public utility services.

6. Directors, Alternate Directors, officers and employees of the Bank shall be subject to an internal effective tax for the benefit of the Bank on salaries and emoluments paid by the Bank, subject to conditions to be laid down and rules to be adopted by the Board of Governors within a period of one year from the date of entry into force of this Agreement. From the date on which this tax is applied, such salaries and emoluments shall be exempt from national income tax. The members may, however, take into account the salaries and emoluments thus exempt when assessing the amount of tax to be applied to income from other sources.

7. Notwithstanding the provisions of paragraph 6 of this Article, a member may deposit, with its instrument of ratification, acceptance or approval, a declaration that such member retains for itself, its political subdivisions or its local authorities the right to tax salaries and emoluments paid by the Bank to citizens or nationals of such member. The Bank shall be exempt from any obligations for the payment, withholding or collection of such taxes. The Bank shall not make any reimbursement for such taxes.

8. Paragraph 6 of this Article shall not apply to pensions and annuities paid by the Bank.

9. No tax of any kind shall be levied on any obligation or security issued by the Bank, including any dividend or interest thereon, by whomsoever held:

(i) which discriminates against such obligation or security solely because it is issued by the Bank, or

(ii)   if the sole jurisdictional basis for such taxation is the place or currency in which it is issued, made payable or paid, or the location of any office or place of business maintained by the Bank.

10.   No tax of any kind shall be levied on any obligation or security guaranteed by the Bank, including any dividend or interest thereon by whomsoever held:

(i)   which discriminates against such obligation or security solely because it is guaranteed by the Bank, or

(ii)   if the sole jurisdictional basis for such taxation is the location of any office or place of business maintained by the Bank.

Article 54

IMPLEMENTATION OF CHAPTER

Each member shall promptly take such action as is necessary for the purpose of implementing the provisions of this Chapter and shall inform the Bank of the detailed action which it has taken.

Article 55

WAIVER OF IMMUNITIES, PRIVILEGES AND EXEMPTIONS

The immunities, privileges and exemptions conferred under this Chapter are granted in the interest of the Bank. The Board of Directors may waive to such extent and upon such conditions as it may determine any of the immunities, privileges and exemptions conferred under this Chapter in cases where such action would, in its opinion, be appropriate in the best interests of the Bank. The President shall have the right and the duty to waive any immunity, privilege or exemption in respect of any officer, employee or expert of the Bank, other than the President or a Vice-President, where, in his or her opinion, the immunity, privilege or exemption would impede the course of justice and can be waived without prejudice to the interests of the Bank. In similar circumstances and under the same conditions, the Board of Directors shall have the right and the duty to waive any immunity, privilege or exemption in respect of the President and each Vice-President.

Chapter IX

AMENDMENTS, INTERPRETATION, ARBITRATION

Article 56

AMENDMENTS

1. Any proposals to amend this Agreement, whether emanating from a member, a Governor or the Board of Directors, shall be communicated to the Chairman of the Board of Governors who shall bring the proposal before the Board. If the proposed amendment is approved by the Board the Bank shall, by any rapid means of communication, ask all members whether they accept the proposed amendment. When not less than three-fourths of the members (including at least two countries from Central and Eastern Europe listed in Annex A), having not less than four-fifths of the total voting power of the members, have accepted the proposed amendment, the Bank shall certify that fact by formal communication addressed to all members.

2. Notwithstanding paragraph 1 of this Article:

   (i)   acceptance by all members shall be required in the case of any amendment modifying:
   (a)   the right to withdraw from the Bank;
   (b)   the rights pertaining to purchase of capital stock provided for in paragraph 3 of Article 5 of this Agreement;
   (c)   the limitation on liability provided for in paragraph 7 of Article 5 of this Agreement; and
   (d)   the purpose and functions of the Bank defined by Articles 1 and 2 of this Agreement;
   (ii) acceptance by not less than three-fourths of the members having not less than eighty-five (85) percent of the total voting power of the members shall

be required in the case of any amendment modifying paragraph 4 of Article 8 of this Agreement.

When the requirements for accepting any such proposed amendment have been met, the Bank shall certify that fact by formal communication addressed to all members.

3.   Amendments shall enter into force for all members three (3) months after the date of the formal communication provided for in paragraphs 1 and 2 of this Article unless the Board of Governors specifies a different period.

Article 57

INTERPRETATION AND APPLICATION

1.   Any question of interpretation or application of the provisions of this Agreement arising between any member and the Bank, or between any members of the Bank, shall be submitted to the Board of Directors for its decision. If there is no Director of its nationality in that Board, a member particularly affected by the question under consideration shall be entitled to direct representation in the meeting of the Board of Directors during such consideration. The representative of such member shall, however, have no vote. Such right of representation shall be regulated by the Board of Governors.

2.   In any case where the Board of Directors has given a decision under paragraph 1 of this Article, any member may require that the question be referred to the Board of Governors, whose decision shall be final. Pending the decision of the Board of Governors, the Bank may, so far as it deems it necessary, act on the basis of the decision of the Board of Directors.

Article 58

ARBITRATION

If a disagreement should arise between the Bank and a member which has ceased to be a member, or between the Bank and any member after adoption of a decision to terminate the operations of the Bank, such disagreement shall be submitted to arbitration by a tribunal of three (3) arbitrators, one appointed by the Bank, another by the member or former member concerned, and the third, unless the parties otherwise agree, by the President of the International Court of Justice or such other authority as may have been prescribed by regulations adopted by the Board of Governors. A majority vote of the arbitrators shall be sufficient to reach a decision which shall be final and binding upon the parties. The third arbitrator shall have full power to settle all questions of procedure in any case where the parties are in disagreement with respect thereto.

Article 59

APPROVAL DEEMED GIVEN

Whenever the approval or the acceptance of any member is required before any act may be done by the Bank, except under Article 56 of this Agreement, approval or acceptance shall be deemed to have been given unless the member presents an objection within such reasonable period as the Bank may fix in notifying the member of the proposed act.

Chapter X

FINAL PROVISION

Article 60

SIGNATURE AND DEPOSIT

1. This Agreement, deposited with the Government of the French Republic (hereinafter called "the Depository"), shall remain open until 31 December 1990 for signature by the prospective members whose names are set forth in Annex A to this Agreement.

2. The Depository shall communicate certified copies of this Agreement to all the Signatories.

Article 61

RATIFICATION, ACCEPTANCE OR APPROVAL

1.   The Agreement shall be subject to ratification, acceptance or approval by the Signatories. Instruments of ratification, acceptance or approval shall, subject to paragraph 2 of this Article, be deposited with the Depository not later than 31 March 1991. The Depository shall duly notify the other Signatories of each deposit and the date thereof.

2.   Any Signatories may become a party to this Agreement by depositing an instrument of ratification, acceptance or approval until one year after the date of its entry into force or, if necessary, until such later date as may be decided by a majority of Governors, representing a majority of the total voting power of the members.

3.   A Signatory whose instrument referred to in paragraph 1 of this Article is deposited before the date on which this Agreement enters into force shall become a member of the Bank on that date. Any other Signatory which complies with the provisions of the preceding paragraph shall become a member of the Bank on the date on which its instrument of ratification, acceptance or approval is deposited.

Article 62

ENTRY INTO FORCE

1.   This Agreement shall enter into force when instruments of ratification, acceptance or approval have been deposited by Signatories whose initial subscriptions represent not less than two-thirds of the total subscriptions set forth in Annex A, including at least two countries from Central and Eastern Europe listed in Annex A.

2.   If this Agreement has not entered into force by 31 March 1991, the Depository may convene a conference of interested prospective members to determine the future course of action and decide a new date by which instruments of ratification, acceptance or approval shall be deposited.

Article 63

INAUGURAL MEETING AND COMMENCEMENT OF OPERATIONS

1.   As soon as this Agreement enters into force under Article 62 of this Agreement, each member shall appoint a Governor. The Depository shall call the first meeting of the Board of Governors within sixty (60) days of entry into force of this Agreement under Article 62 or as soon as possible thereafter.

2.   At its first meeting, the Board of Governors:

    (i)   shall elect the President;

    (ii) shall elect the Directors of the Bank in accordance with Article 26 of this Agreement;

    (iii) shall make arrangements for determining the date of the commencement of the Bank's operations; and

    (iv) shall make such other arrangements as appear to it necessary to prepare for the commencement of the Bank's operations.

3.   The Bank shall notify its members of the date of commencement of its operations.

Done at Paris on 29 May 1990 in a single original, whose English, French, German and Russian texts are equally authentic, which shall be deposited in the archives of the Depository which shall transmit a duly certified copy to each of the other prospective members whose names are set forth in Annex A.

Source: EBRD/Agreement establishing the European Bank for Reconstruction and Development.

Appendix 5

List of names and previous functions of the members of the Board of Directors

share-holder	share	director	previous function
single constituencies:			
United States	10.0%	Mrs. E. Walker *)	Executive Secretary Department of Treasury
France	8.5175%	Mr. P. Mordacq	Chief Executive Commission des Operations de Bourse, Paris
F.R. of Germany	8.5175%	Mr. G. Winkelmann	Division Chief in the Federal Ministry of Finance
Italy	8.5175%	Mr. G. Maresca	General Directorate of the Treasury
Japan	8.5175%	Mr. S. Miyake **)	Financial Minister Embassy of Japan, London
United Kingdom	8.5175%	Mr J.A.L. Faint	Under Secretary, Overseas Development Administration
Soviet Union	6.0%	Mr. A.S. Maslov	Director, Moscow Narodny Bank
Eur. Community	3.0%	Mr. A. van Goethem	Director for Finance, Commission of the European Communities
Eur. Inv. Bank	3.0%	Mr. C. Sibson	Head of Division, EIB
Netherlands	2.48%	Mr. R. Keller	Head of Multilateral Banks Division Ministry of Finance
multiple constituencies:			
Spain Mexico	3.70%	Mr. J.L. Ugarte (S)	

Canada Morocco	3.5%	Mr. D.M. McCutchan (C)	Chief of Staff to Finance Ministry
Switzerland Turkey Liechtenstein	3.45%	Mr. N. Imboden (S)	Deputy Chief, World Trade and GATT Division Swiss Federal Office for Foreign Economic Affairs
Austria Cyprus Israël Malta	3.04%	Mr. H. Luschin (A)	Director Federal Ministry of Finance
Finland Norway	2.5%	Mr. K. Nars (F)	Director of Finance Ministry of Finance
Belgium Luxembourg	2.48%	Mr. G. Noppen (B)	Inspector General of the Foreign Department of the NBB, Brussels
Sweden Iceland	2.38%	Mr. C. de Neergard (S)	Managing Director Nordbanken Luxembourg
Poland Bulgaria	2.07%	Mr. J. Winiecki (P)	Associate Professor School of Social Sciences Aalborg University Denmark
Czechoslovakia Hungary	2.07%	Mr. T. Parizek (C)	Director CSFR/State Bank
Australia Egypt South Korea New Zealand	1.85%	Mr. J. Humphreys (A)	High Commissioner for Australia in Canada
Yugoslavia Romania	1.76%	Mr. B. Pajkovic (Y)	Federal Executive Council
Denmark Ireland	1.50%	Mr. L. Tybjerg (D)	Assistant Permanent Secretary Financial Affairs Ministry of Finance
Portugal Greece	1.07%	Mr. J. da Silva Lopes (P)	Member of the Committee on the Reform of the Financial System, Lisbon

Note: In the period April–July 1991 the following changes took place:
*) Alternate Director; appointment by the Governor of the United States of a Director for the United States: Mr. W.G. Curran;
**) Appointment by the Governor of Japan of a new Director for Japan: Mr. T. Fujikawa.

Source: EBRD/Press Release dated 19 April 1991.

Appendix 6

Role of the various organisational units of the EBRD

UNIT	ACTIVITIES
Merchant Banking	Finance and advise all autonomous companies and financial institutions (ie all enterprises run in a commercially independent fashion)
	Develop and help to execute restructuring and privatisation plans which create commercially autonomous companies
	Finance and advise all commercially autonomous financial intermediaries
	Finance the small business sector through the medium of domestic financial institutions
Development Banking	Manage overall Bank relationship with government
	Review country economic position and changing priorities
	Develop strategy for the Bank in each country
	Advise on and develop projects focused on overall financial infra-structure reform
	Develop programmes for enhancement of publicly owned infrastructure and cross-border 'master plans' for key sectors
	Create and execute financing and advisory projects to develop infrastructure
	Provide a pool of specific technical capabilities which support projects and programmes eg Training support; Management of Co-operation Fund relationships; Technical assistance administration.
Finance	Responsibility for all the Bank's finances, including: - treasury functions, management of capital, borrowing and capital market transactions; - establishing financial and accounting policies and controls; - budgeting, planning, and performance monitoring, including the provision of supporting information technology system; - assist quality review: • policies and procedures for credit and investment review;

	• appraisal of Operations Department's proposals for fit with these policies; – asset and liability risk management.
Personnel and Administration	Conducting or subcontracting basic administrative activities (property management, transport, mail, etc). Defining and executing the Bank's human resources strategy in support of attracting, motivating and retaining high quality staff. Monitoring the application of employment policies and regulations. Planning and executing staff recruitment and development programmes. Implementing the compensation and benefits packages.
Evaluation	Responsible for the development of post-completion evaluation studies of the Bank, to help improve the design and conduct of Bank activities in the future and the effective use of resources.
Chief Economist's Office	Provision of general economic advisory service to the Operations Departments, focusing on high level insights on the economics of transition: – development of high quality reports which guide internal thinking and establish the intellectual leadership of the Bank on key aspects of policy making; – sharing economic information with other international economic and financial institutions. Developing appropriate economic analysis throughout the Bank
General Counsel's Office	Advice and assistance to the Board of Governors, Board of Directors, management and Operations Departments on legal issues.
Secretary General's Office	Liaison function between management and the Board, providing inter alia: – Board's Activity Plans; – administrative and secretarial support to the Board; – information service; – cooperation agreements with international institutions.
Internal Audit	Assistance to the management with periodic independent and objective appraisals and audits of financial accounting, administrative and other activities.
Press and Communications	Responsible for public affairs relations with various audiences, as well as providing accurate and timely information to the news media.

Source: EBRD/Memorandum on the overall organisation of the Bank, 23 March 1991.

Appendix 7

EBRD policy paper Operational Challenges and Priorities: Initial Orientations; Part two – Priorities

Overall Priorities: Main Areas and Sectors

The Bank's operational priorities spring from its view of conditions necessary for successful reform in the Central and Eastern European countries as described above, taking into account assistance provided by other organisations.

It is premature at this stage, when there is still much work and analysis to be done, to lock the Bank into any rigid course of action. However, there are a number of fundamental priorities which can already be identified to guide the Bank's choice of operational objectives. In particular, but not in any rank order, the Bank will place initial emphasis on programmes and activities that support:

- the creation or strengthening of infrastructure necessary for private sector development and the transition to a market economy, including institutional infrastructure (regulatory, communications and services) and physical infrastructure (telecommunications, transportation and energy);

- privatisation;
- reform of the financial sector, including restructuring of existing banks, the creation of new financial intermediaries, the development of capital markets and the privatisation of the commercial banking sector;
- the development of a productive, competitive private sector, including small and medium-sized companies in industry, agriculture and services;
- restructuring of industrial enterprises and subsectors to operate competitively;
- the stimulation of foreign direct investment;
- environmental rehabilitation.

The Bank must include these basic market economy building-blocks in its priorities. Many of these will necessitate difficult and time-consuming preparatory steps, essential for the development of the human and institutional base without which a market-based economic system cannot function.

Many *other areas of potential involvement for the Bank* could contribute to the success of the reform process. They include urban renovation and transportation, public utilities, rural development, agriculture, health care and education. Municipal services are an area where the Bank might take an active role as they receive relatively limited support from multilateral and bilateral organisations. Housing will also be important because it can be a lever for necessary social changes.

The Bank will not be able, nor does it expect to take a leading role in all of the areas indicated. Rather, it expects to respond to country needs progressively in a manner that is commensurate with the growth of its own experience and expertise. The Bank must take account of the activities and programmes of other multilateral and bilateral organisations in the countries and functional areas in which it will be operating. It will plan to take a central role in some areas (such as privatisation, restructuring, etc.), while in others it will co-finance with other organisations. The latter would, among other things, permit the Bank to husband its resources while increasing its multiplier effect.

The Bank will concentrate its efforts on developing an entrepreneurial spirit at grass roots level by helping the establishment of small enterprises and by supporting their development through the financial infrastructure that the Bank will also promote and support. The Bank will prepare country-specific strategies in order to refine country priorities and the most suitable Bank programmes to achieve them.

The Bank's Specificity

Against that background, what in particular does the European Bank have to offer that is different from other sources of assistance?

The Agreement establishing the European Bank provides the answer. The Bank is the only international financial institution that has a specific brief to focus on Central and Eastern European countries which have embraced multiparty democracy, in order to help their transition to market economies. All of these elements in its mandate are vital – the region on which to focus, the political aspects of that focus and the economic doctrine that must be followed (competition, privatisation and openness to foreign investment). Thus the first original feature of the European Bank is its mandate.

Secondly, from that mandate inevitably follows the approach which the European Bank must take. It must have an advisory relationship with Central and Eastern European governments. This is not to substitute for the advice of other international financial institutions; it is clear from the Agreement that this will not happen. But the Bank would clearly be failing in its duty if it did not express its views on political and economic reform in these countries. The required annual reviews of country performance by the Bank's Board cannot usefully take place without close dialogue and understanding between the Bank and its member countries of operations.

Third, the Bank must also, according to its Agreement, make use of a range of traditional public assistance and modern banking methods, other than quick disbursing policy-based lending and insurance in order to facilitate change. This is the first time an international financial institution has housed all of these different tools under one roof, thereby giving it the capacity for flexibility, efficiency and rapidity. Many of the Bank's priority activities will require it to operate effectively both at government and enterprise level. This is particularly true for financial sector reform, privatisation and restructuring. It will also be the case for infrastructure development, where private investors will be called upon to play a significant role. For these activities, the European Bank will be in a strong position to provide effective assistance through a balanced mix of public and private sector skills and a flexible portfolio of financial instruments (ability to provide equity and debt, and in the latter case with and without government guarantees).

Fourth, it is the first international institution that has a clear mandate on environmental protection and restoration, a matter of major importance for the Central and Eastern European region and its neighbours.

The European Bank is the only institution dedicated solely to the priorities mentioned above and to the Central and Eastern European countries. This focus, together with the Bank's physical proximity to its countries of operations, offer it a unique opportunity to take the intellectual lead in developing fresh ideas concerning the complex issues of economic restructuring in the region.

The new instituion will bring a *special European dimension* to its activities. Many of the issues confronting Central and European countries (e.g. environmental pollution, immigration, agricultural development, industrial restructuring) will have a direct impact on Europe as a whole. The European Bank will thus become a leading participant in pan-European discussions on economic issues.

Operational decisions will be made against the background of country-specific strategies, on which the European Bank will work further in the months ahead. The Bank will not be involved in every sector from the beginning, but the descriptions below show the possibilities, subject to country strategy decisions.

Creating Modern Infrastructure

The European Bank will have a special role to play in supporting infrastructure projects necessary for private sector development and the transition to a market-oriented economy. Other bilateral and multilateral sources will also be heavily involved in financing such operations.

The Bank will cooperate very closely with the European Economic Community, the European Investment Bank (EIB), the World Bank and individual governments and organisations in promoting infrastructure-related projects (transport, telecommunications, energy, housing, municipal services and environmental rehabilitation). It will also strive to develop innovative approaches to infrastructure development, giving priority attention to projects which can make a significant contribution to regional integration.

The Bank will concentrate initially on a few key pre-investment programmes of regional significance and on priority infrastructural investments already identified. In both cases, the Bank will operate closely with other international financial institutions, either as a co-manager of pre-investment/technical assistance programmes, or as a co-financer of specific investment projects. Co-financing opportunities with the EIB, the Nordic Investment Bank (NIB) and the World Bank will be considered in the coming months.

Two characteristics of the infrastructure challenge will condition the Bank's approach:

(i) institutional strengthening, policy reforms and managerial support will be essential elements. This will call for massive technical assistance and advisory services from the Bank in addition to the direct financing of specific projects;

(ii) innovative approaches to foster public/private sector partnerships in infrastructure financing and management will be needed, such as Build, Operate and Transfer schemes in transportation and energy and the participation of foreign operators in telecommunications. The Bank will be ideally placed to assist country and local authorities in attracting capital and managerial expertise from private operators on a long-term contractural basis.

(i) Energy

Energy issues are among the most important needing to be addressed by decision-makers in the context of the overall reforms now under way in the countries of operations. As described above, the structural transition called for transcends the energy production and consuming sectors.

A regional initiative (the Eastern and Central Europe Regional Energy Programme) is under consideration by the countries concerned. This programme would provide technical assistance to facilitate the preparation of strategies and priority investments for energy production, trade, efficiency improvement and energy-related environmental management. The Programme would result in considerable benefits for the operations and their neighbours: faster and more appropriate policy reforms, more effective institutional adjustments, better prepared investment programmes and projects, economic gains from optimal energy trade, and better co-ordinated strategies and assistance programmes in the energy field. The Bank intends to play an active role in the design and execution of this regional programme.

(ii) Telecommunications

The Bank will examine in further detail in the coming months the possibility of establishing with other interested institutions a regional telecommunications programme along the lines of that proposed for the energy sector, with the following priorities:

- reform of the corporate structure and performance of telecommunications agencies (separation from governments and postal activities, transformation into commercial enterprises, introduction of management and financial systems emphasising efficiency and customer responsiveness, etc.);
- financing network expansion and modernisation (transformation of telecommunications into a self-supporting activity, internal cash generation, subscribers' contributions, reorientation towards high return services, etc.);
- technology (options for modernising the network in the special circumstances of Central and Eastern Europe; role of optical, satellite, mobile, digital overlay networks, digital islands, etc.);
- privatisation prospects (role of alternative service providers: private networks, mobile carriers, independent local carriers; role of outside capital joint ventures with foreign companies, municipal and cooperative systems, etc.);
- regulation (regulatory structure to manage complex and commercialised telecommunications tariffs, interconnection, electromagnetic spectrum, franchises, accounting and disclosure, etc.).

The Bank will also explore individual cofinancing possibilities for the few telecommunications projects which are currently being considered by some countries of operations.

(iii) Transport

In view of the capital intensity of this sector and the magni-

tude of the task, it will be essential for the Bank clearly to focus
its assistance. In particular, the fiscal relationship between
transport infrastructure investments and the macroeconomy is
too strong to allow duplication or inappropriate choices of
technology or service standards. In addition, the financial
dependency of the local governments involved on central budgets and the corresponding need for a comprehensive reform of
local taxation systems to accompany the decentralisation process, call for a cautious and highly prioritised approach by the
Bank.

The European Bank will concentrate in the first instance on
transport infrastructure projects which would eliminate severe
bottlenecks to the development of the competitive sector: rehabilitation of existing infrastructure, completion of economically viable unfinished projects and development of essential
inter-regional networks.

(iv) Municipal Services

The main rationale for involvement of the Bank in municipal
services development and urban management support stems
from the close relationship between the productivity of the
urban economy and the overall growth prospects in the
countries of operations. As these countries gradually move to a
market-based economy, urban economic activities will make up
an increasing share of GDP and constraints on productivity in
the urban sector may constitute a severe impediment to private
sector development in both the industrial and service sectors.

In addition, several trends, including political decentralisation and the social significance of urban environmental issues,
indicate that local governments will play a growing role in economic development. Issues of managing decentralisation, local
fiscal resources mobilization and improved planning and management of key municipal services, will be central preoccupations
for the Bank.

The assistance strategy of the Bank will therefore focus on the
following elements:

- strengthening the management of urban infrastructure at
  the city level by helping to improve the level and composition of investment, reinforcing the institutional capacity for
  operation and maintenance and seeking opportunities for
  greater private sector involvement;

- helping to improve the city-wide regulatory framework to increase market efficiency and to enhance the private sector's provision of municipal services;
- strengthening financial services for urban development.

In undertaking these activities, the Bank will develop strong links with local constituencies. Given its core mandate and its small size, the Bank will however need to concentrate its efforts on those local authorities with whom true partnerships can be developed.

The Bank will also need to develop mechanisms to disseminate its experience in urban management, so as to encourage replication at the regional level.

(v) Housing

Housing reform will be an important lever of economic and social policy during the transition to a market economy. First, housing subsidies have a large, direct impact on national budgets. Second, the sector could become a major instrument in the mobilization of household savings. Third, the provision of housing by enterprises places a serious economic burden on enterprises, and significantly reduces labour mobility.

Because of the significant role of the housing sector in the economy, the massive amount of subsidies it receives, the largely regressive nature of these subsidies and the very distorted pricing of rental housing, reforms in all of the countries of operations are of the highest priority. Reforms needed range from property rights and rent reform to privatisation of the existing housing stock and to the development of a housing finance system (new institutions and new long-term lending instruments). Diversification of the housing industry will also be essential to eliminate housing shortages and to create sound employment.

The Bank will have to explore within the next few months how it could best support the creation of housing markets in its countries of operations. Housing finance, which might in itself be a tool for developing the banking sector and support for diversification of the housing industry, seem to be the most promising areas for intervention.

(vi) Environmental Management

In line with the provisions of its Agreement, the Bank will

place environmental management at the forefront of its operations to promote sustainable economic growth in the region. It is already involved in the Baltic Sea Task Force through its contribution to some of the studies being undertaken and its role as a member of the Steering Group. To a large extent, environmental management issues will be addressed through the range of infrastructure related projects outlined above. In addition, the Bank intends to provide direct assistance to its countries of operations in environmental policy formulation and in the development of an environmental goods and services industry. The Bank will also promote special regional programmes to address the transboundary nature of air and water pollution on the European continent.

Strengthening Financial Institutions

In this area the Bank will span a broad spectrum of activities, from general advice to governments on the structure of the financial sector to the financing of specific financial intermediaries.

(i) Advice to Governments on Financial Institutions Reforms

The Bank will play an active role in this process by providing advice through its own staff and by financing experts through technical assistance. Many fundamental decisions about the structure of the financial sector still need to be made. The basic legal framework also needs to be defined and supervisory bodies close to the main European models need to be put in place. The Bank will need to coordinate closely with other institutions such as the European Communities, the Bank for International Settlements and the World Bank to avoid overlap and to ensure consistency of advice.

(ii) Restructuring of Existing Banks

The assistance the Bank can provide includes:

- financing expert advice to specific banks to assist in modernising their operations, developing new strategies and cleaning up their balance sheets;
- the provision of lines of credit to increase the lending capacity

of those restructured banks (or in many cases their off-shoots) which have a sound balance sheet;
- the provision of subordinated loans or equity to improve capitalisation ratios;
- financing training programmes designed to improve modern credit evaluation and banking skills. In addition the Bank could play a key coordination role in helping local banks secure foreign partners or strategic investors;
- participation in, or support for, the privatisation of existing state-owned commercial banks.

(iii) Creation of New Financial Intermediaries

The Bank intends to play a significant role by being a catalyst for the creation of these new intermediaries, mainly involving the private sector, and has already initiated advisory work on two potential projects in the USSR and the CSFR. Specifically the Bank could:

(i) help local institutions and financial entrepreneurs develop detailed strategies and feasibility studies for the launching of new initiatives;

(ii) find foreign partners to assist in these;

(iii) provide seed capital, thereby acting as a catalyst to attract other equity investors; and

(iv) provide lines of credit.

Special mention should be made of the creation of local merchant banks. The European Bank should have a special role here as such banks could become an efficient way of providing its financial and advisory assistance to the local private sector. Ultimately, the European Bank should aim to create a network of such institutions spanning the entire region.

(iv) Development of Capital Markets

All countries wishing to modernise their financial infrastructure need to develop their securities markets. Typically this starts with the creation of government and/or corporate fixed income securities market evolving gradually to an equity market. Great emphasis has been put on the immediate development of the stock market, thus short-circuiting the normal process. As there are significant risks in premature development of capital markets, the Bank will want to assist governments and local financial authorities in the overall planning of capital markets development; in setting up adequate legal and regulatory frameworks and in the institutional building effort. While much of this advice is already being provided by a number of experts, the Bank has a special role to play because of its broader perspective and the greater caution that it might want to exercise.

Beyond advice, the European Bank will be able to help provide liquidity and depth to these emerging capital markets in a variety of ways:

- assistance in the creation and/or financing of local institutional investors;
- direct participation in local capital markets (underwriting, investment on its own account, market-making);
- encouragement of foreign participation in local capital markets through active marketing, through dissemination of market information and securities research and through the exercise of overall leadership in the market.

Developing the Local Private Sector

Virtually all of the Bank's activities will be aimed at supporting directly or indirectly the creation of a prosperous local private sector. In addition to its involvement in privatisation, restructuring and foreign investment, the Bank will participate directly in the development of the local private sector by supporting local businesses of various scales, in agriculture, industry and the service sector.

A very important aspect of the Bank's mission is to foster an entrepreneurial culture in its countries of operations. Most private sector projects will contribute to this goal but the Bank will focus its efforts on projects directly supporting private entrepreneurs. In that context the Bank aims also to support appropriate management buy-outs.

(i) Small Enterprises
The Bank will not support small enterprises directly, for reasons of cost efficiency. Rather it will concentrate its efforts on creating the conditions under which small entrepreneurs can thrive, in particular through the development and financing of financial intermediaries geared to assist small businesses. The Bank will also contribute to the creation of local advisory firms which can assist entrepreneurs in developing viable projects. It has already

initiated one such venture, in collaboration with the IFC, to which it is planning to second staff.

The Bank will also be providing support indirectly to small businesses through its assistance to large scale enterprises which would support the growth of a multitude of smaller businesses. The 'trickle down' effect has not to be disregarded as a potential boost to the creation of smaller businesses. In the case of restructuring, the Bank will work with the enterprises being restructured to explore ways in which such enterprises can directly encourage the creation of smaller businesses through employee spin-offs and sub-contracting.

(ii) Local Company Financing

The European Bank will seek to identify local private sector companies of sufficient size and quality to warrant direct support in the form of equity and debt financing, as well as advice. From the outset the Bank expects to have heavy demands from local companies seeking advice, in particular on the identification of and negotiations with foreign partners. The Bank's financing of local ventures without foreign participation will be limited, however, because of the difficulty of assessing the performance of local managers and the extensive resources required to evaluate such projects.

As the Bank builds its own expertise and as it becomes better established in its countries of operations, in particular through the establishment of local offices, it will be in a position to expand these operations which will eventually account for a substantial portion of the Bank's portfolio.

Implementing Privatisation

The Bank is already participating in privatisation work in Hungary, Poland and Bulgaria. At this stage and for the immediate future its participation is limited to providing overall programme advice. The importance of obtaining concessionary funding to finance such advice is paramount. In addition, and in response to the immediate demands of several countries, the Bank is already working to develop financial intermediaries. The following is an overview of a broader range of activities in which the Bank plans to engage as its staff and expertise grow.

(i) Overall Programme Advice

Working independently or in conjunction with other advisors, the European Bank will provide advice to governments on the overall content of their privatisation programmes. The advice will take a number of forms and will draw upon experience gained from the Bank's involvement in transactions and processes in the region. These might include advising on the definition of a sound overall strategy; development of a legislative framework and preparation of a realistic work programme. Advice will be given on the most appropriate techniques for privatisation; joint ventures; trade sales; leases; management contracts and management/employee buy-outs. The Bank might also play a role in prioritising the entities for privatisation by helping to identify a portfolio of groups of enterprises from existing state conglomerations.

Apart from acting as an advisor in its own right, the Bank will also provide assistance to the countries of operations on selection, coordination and management of other advisors. The Bank will help to mobilize and identify key experts as well as to identify possible external sources for their funding. When appropriate it will also act as a lead advisor, subcontracting tasks to other advisors. Throughout, the Bank will strive to ensure that the governments involved receive objective services which meet their needs.

(ii) Specific Enterprise Advice

The Bank will also be involved in providing advice for specific transactions. As with programme advice, this will take the two forms of acting as an advisor itself and of coordinating others' advice. When acting as an advisor the Bank will naturally act for the seller, so as to avoid any conflicts with the Bank's programme advisory role before privatisation. The Bank's coordination of other advisors will be most important in relation to the restructuring of state enterprises. For the privatisation itself, again usually working with other advisors, the Bank will help review valuations, techniques and proposed strategies. In all these transactions the Bank's added value will be to concentrate on precedent-setting transactions to be used as models for the future.

(iii) Setting-up Intermediaries

International advisors, including the Bank, will play an important role in many of the major privatisations. However, the need for domestic intermediaries, not least to participate in smaller privatisations, is paramount. These intermediaries can broadly be divided into two categories: those providing financial purchasing mechanisms and those providing advice.

The Bank will provide help in a number of areas. It will identify which type of institutions are needed (i.e. investment funds, banks or other intermediaries). It will help in preparing feasibility studies and advise on the structuring of these institutions and on mobilizing management expertise. The Bank will also be ready to provide funding as well as seed equity. For some intermediaries, such as merchant banks, the Bank might help by seconding some of its own professionals in the start-up period.

(iv) Participation as a Core Investor

In addition to investing in financial intermediaries, the Bank will also invest in selected privatisations. Such investment will encourage other international investors. When taking an equity stake the Bank will, in line with its founding Agreement, not take a controlling position but will nonetheless seek to provide necessary longer term stability to the enterprise and to play a constructive role in management through representation on the Board whenever appropriate. The Bank will divest its equity once it feels that it has added all the value it can, and once the equity can be sold on appropriate terms, so as to recycle it productively, in line with provisions in the Agreement establishing the Bank.

Restructuring the Industrial Sector

Restructuring the industrial sector will be a long and complicated process. Although the Bank's principal role here will be to provide finance, initially it will focus on providing limited advice on overall strategies and the restructuring of a few selected industries and enterprises. Progressively, as the Bank develops its own expertise, it will broaden its role to include the full range of activities outlined below.

(i) Overall Programme Advice

In parallel to the advice provided to governments on privatisation, the European Bank also plans to advise governments on restructuring issues. Whilst this could cover a broad range of subjects (e.g. overall strategy, work programmes, establishing of priorities), the Bank will concentrate on areas where it is able to provide the most added value. Because of its European focus, these will include the development of regional strategies to restructure specific industrial sectors, as well as advice on external trade and industrial policy issues, in coordination with other relevant international institutions. For many of these advisory activities, in particular those which require extensive resources (such as the preparation of sector specific industrial strategies), the Bank will act as general contractor and subcontract the bulk of the detailed work to specialized consulting firms.

(ii) Specific Enterprise Advice

When dealing with specific restructuring operations the Bank will aim to work directly with the enterprise. In doing so, it will usually help mobilize and coordinate a team of experts (management consultants, engineering and financial advisory firms) and will limit its direct involvement in detailed issues. It will, however, have a special role to play in the dialogue with senior management over the implementation of the recommendations and an active role in discussions between the restructured enterprise and the government.

(iii) Financing

The financing assistance that the Bank can provide in the area of industrial restructuring will be at two levels. First, to help the government finance some of the costs for which the government will have to take responsibility, such as retraining. Second, to help finance or refinance enterprises in the process of being restructured. This could involve financing of new physical assets or the rehabilitation of existing ones. It might also involve providing a working capital finance facility or equity in order to recapitalize the balance sheet.

Encouraging Foreign Direct Investment

The Bank has a clear mandate to stimulate foreign direct investment. To achieve this it will combine advisory, promotional and financing activities.

Assisting local companies to find foreign opartners and investors, as well as assisting foreign companies to find local partners, will be a central activity of the Merchant Banking Department. The need for such a service is apparent from the various requests already received by the Bank. The Bank will have a special role because of its neutrality.

Active promotion of investment opportunities will also be important. This will be done through a variety of means, including provision to foreign companies of information on local conditions and market opportunities and, above all, the maintenance of a close dialogue with senior foreign executives and the provision to them of informal advice, market information and contacts in Central and Eastern European countries.

Participation by the Bank in the equity of a venture will raise considerably the level of comfort to other foreign participants, by helping to overcome their concerns related to country and political risks. European Bank loan financing will, in many cases, be essential, as this is likely to be one of the only sources of non-recourse financing in most, if not all, of its countries of operations for the forseeable future. In addition and in due course, the Bank will evaluate whether other forms of financial involvement (such as specially tailored guarantees) could add to the Bank's effectiveness as a catalyst for generating direct investment flows.

Technical Assistance, Training and Advisory Services

The magnitude of the technical assistance as well as the training effort required in the Bank's countries of operations is evident from the above discussion of the challenges facing them. Both technical assistance and training will be at the core of most of the Bank's activities and will be provided in virtually all of the Bank's projects.

The Bank will also, over time, develop and support 'stand-alone' training programmes, both in the region and its headquarters. These training programmes could cover a broad range of subjects, including enterprise management, banking (in particular credit evaluation), public sector management and project development and evaluation. The Bank will also play a role in helping universities in the countries of operations to reorganise their programmes and to create links with foreign universities.

The scope and precise nature of the Bank's training programmes will depend to a large extent on the concessionary funding provided by the Bank. Some governments have already announced such funding to the Bank for this purpose, on top of their capital subscriptions. Others will do so shortly.

In addition, the Bank will try to reach cooperation agreements with the many bilateral and multilateral assistance programmes for Central and Eastern Europe which already exist. Some governments and the European Communities have already indicated their intention to make available some of their technical assistance funds for European Bank projects.

Source: EBRD/Operational Challenges and Priorities: Initial Orientations, April 1991, pp. 12–20.

References and notes

Chapter 2

1. Purpose of the European Bank for Reconstruction and Development as formulated in article 1 of the Agreement establishing the EBRD. The preamble and articles of the Agreement are reproduced in appendix 4.
2. J.E. Spero, *The Politics of International Economic Relations*, fourth edition (London, 1990), section 'The Creation of an Eastern Economic Bloc', pp. 306-310.
3. According to B. Milanovic, *Liberalization and Entrepreneurship* (New York, 1989): size of the state sector measured by output and employment varied in centrally planned economies from 65-97% resp. 70-95%, compared to market-oriented economies 1-16% resp. 2-20%.
4. *Financial Times*, 'The dog that failed to bark', 10 January 1989.
5. The following part of this section borrows extensively from in this context relevant parts in J.M.C. Rollo, *The New Eastern Europe: Western Responses* (London, 1990), pp. 6-62.
6. Federigo Argentieri, 'East-Central Europe', in *The International Spectator*, Volume XXV, No. 4 October-December 1990, pp. 261-267.
7. *International Herald Tribune*, 'A Chance to Transform Communism Into Democracy', 7 July 1989.
8. IMF publication, SN/89/202, 5 October 1989.
9. See Wim F. Duisenberg, 'Marx's Moneymen', in *European Affairs* 3/90.
10. See Lawrence J. Brainard, '*Strategies for Economic Transformation in Eastern Europe/The Role of Financial Market Reform*', Bankers Trust Company (New York, 1990). Also in *Financial Times*, Economics Notebook: 'Capitalism in Eastern Europe', 12 November 1990.
11. See *The Economist*, 22 September 1990, 'A Survey of World Trade', pp. 12-19.
12. Bimal Ghosh, 'Money can't buy reform', in *European Affairs* 3/90, p. 99.
13. J.M.C. Rollo, *The New Eastern Europe: Western Responses* (London, 1990), pp. 69-74.
14. US Treasury Secretary Mr. Brady quoted in the *Financial Times*, 26 March

1990, 'The Eastern bloc countries . . . are counting on our help and . . . come to Washington once a week to ask for our assistance'.

15. Timothy Garton Ash, 'Eastern Europe: Après Le Déluge, Nous', in *The New York Review of Books*, 16 August 1990, Volume XXXVII, nr. 13, pp. 51-57.

16. Central and Eastern Europe's debt per capita and debt (minus reserves) related to exports (in convertible currencies), 1989 (source IMF, OECD): Bulgaria $1050 - 2.6, Czechoslavakia $450 - 1.0, German Democratic Republic $1350 - 1.2, Hungary $1850 -3.3, Poland $1100 - 5.2, Romania $44 - 0.0, Soviet Union $150 - 1.1 and Yugoslavia $750 - 1.1.

17. Paul Krugman, 'Private Capital Flows to Problem Debtors' in Jeffrey D. Sachs, *Developing Country Debt and the World Economy* (Chicago, 1989), pp. 285-289.

18. *Financial Times*, 'E Europe in need of export lifeline', 24 November 1989.

19. Bimal Ghosh, 'Money can't buy reform', in *European Affairs* 3/90, pp. 98-105.

20. J.E. Spero, *The Politics of International Economic Relations*, fourth edition (London, 1990), pp. 319-320. See also *International Herald Tribune*, 'Aiding East: Will U.S. Lead?', 2 October 1989.

21. The International Freedom Foundation (UK) *Opportunities Briefing*, July/August 1990, Nr. 2, p. 2.

22. *Le Monde*, 'Dons, crédits, allégement de dettes . . . à la Hongrie et à la Pologne', 28 November 1989.

23. *Financial Times*, 'Congress approves $938m aid package', 20 November 1989.

24. *Le Monde*, 'Le Japon annonce des aides à la Hongrie et à la Pologne', 25 November 1989.

25. European Currency Unit, ECU 1 billion equals US $1.17 billion (ECU dollar rate December 1989).

26. British Treasury, *Economic Progress Report*, no. 207, April 1990, p. 3.

Chapter 3

1. Darell Delamaide, 'Friends in High Places', in *Euromoney*, June 1990, pp. 24-30. This article also gives a rather lively portrait of Mr. J. Attali. For an extensive curriculum vitae of Mr. Attali see *Le Monde*, 'Jacques Attali, le sherpa de "Dieu"', 22 May 1990.

2. Discours prononcé par monsieur François Mitterrand, Président de la République devant le Parlement Européen à Strasbourg, 25 October 1989, Service de Presse de la Présidence de la République, pp. 18-25.

3. *Bulletin of the European Community*, 10 - 1989, Belgium, November 1989, pp. 79-86.

4. *Frankfurter Allgemeine*, 'Wie kann der Westen helfen?', 10 July 1989.

5. *International Herald Tribune*, 'Eastern Europe: A Job for Planners and Bankers', 5 October 1989.

6. *Le Monde*, 'Qui est le père?', 24 May 1990.

7. A.J.R. Groom, 'The Advent of International Organisation', in Paul Taylor and A.J.R. Groom, *International Institutions At Work* (London, 1990), p. 6.

8. R.P. Barston, *Modern Diplomacy* (London, 1988), pp. 202-203.

9. Harold K. Jacobson, *Networks of Interdependence* (New York, 1979), p. 29.
10. Ibid., p. 44.
11. Herman van der Wee, *Prosperity and Unpheaval* (London, 1986), chapter 11, 'The gold-dollar standard as world system, 1944-1971', pp. 421-478.
12. John H. Jackson, *Restructuring the GATT System* (London, 1990), chapter 2, 'The History and Perspective of GATT', pp. 9-17.
13. Richard N. Gardner, *Stering - dollar diplomacy in current perspective* (New York, 1980), p. xv.
14. James Mayall, 'The Institutional Basis of Post-war Economic Cooperation', in Paul Taylor and A.J.R. Groom, *International Institutions at Work* (London, 1990), pp. 53-74. Poland withdraw and Czechoslovakia was expelled after it failed to complete payment of its subscription.
15. Robert Marjolin, *Architect of European Unity/Memoirs 1911-1986* (London, 1989), p. 182.
16. Viktor V. Gerashchenko, 'Global Economic Institutions: The Russians are coming', in *European Affairs* 3/90, pp. 55-58.
17. Leonard Geron, *Soviet Foreign Economic Policy under Perestroika* (London, 1990), chapter 5, 'The USSR and the International Organisations', pp. 54-64.
18. Harold K. Jacobson, *Networks of Interdependence* (New York, 1979), p. 288.
19. This section is based on the following EIB publications: EIB Annual Report 1989, EIB The European Investment Bank in 1989, EIB Information July 1990 nr. 65 and, EIB Financing in Poland and Hungary, 1990.
20. *Financial Times*, 'France to press proposals for European Development Bank', 1 December 1989.
21. *International Herald Tribune*, 'EC Bank Could Invest Billions in East Bloc', 8 December 1989.
22. *Bulletin of the European Community*, 11 - 1989, Belgium, December 1989, point 2.2.17.
23. Robert Fraser, *The World Financial System*, Keesing's Reference Publications (London, 1987), pp. 297-300.
24. Stefan D. Krasner, *Structural Conflict: the Third World against global liberalism* (Berkeley, 1985), p. 161.
25. *Ibid.*, p. 162.
26. This section is based on the following publications: Robert Fraser, *The World Financial System*, Keesing's Reference Publications (London, 1987), pp. 380-388, World Bank Annual Reports, IFC Annual Reports.
27. EIB Financing in Poland and Hungary, 1990, p. 3.
28. EIB Information. July 1990, nr. 65, p. 4.
29. Darrell Delamaide, 'Friends in High Places', in *Euromoney*, June 1990, pp. 24-30.
30. *Ibid.*
31. Harold K. Jacobson, *Networks of Interdependence* (New York, 1979), pp. 53-54 and 78.
32. According to an article in the *Financial Times*, 'The dog that failed to bark', 10 January 1989, the term 'common house for Europe' is borrowed from Mr. Gromyko.
33. William Diebold, *The Schuman Plan* (Oxford, 1959), pp. 1-2.

34. Robert Marjolin, *Architect of European Unity/Memoirs 1911-1986* (London, 1989), p. 270.
35. Alan James, 'International Institutions: Independent Actors?', in A. Shlaim, *International Organisations in World Politics*, Yearbook 1975 (London, 1976), pp. 77-78.
36. Darell Delamaide, 'Paying the market price', in *Euromoney*, February 1990, pp. 80-86.
37. *Bulletin of the European Community*, 10 - 1989, Belgium, November 1989, pp. 79-86.
38. David S. Yost, 'France in the New Europe', in *Foreign Affairs*, Winter 1990/91, volume 69, nr. 5, 1990, pp. 107-128.
39. J.E. Spero, *The Politics of International Economic Relations*, fourth edition (London, 1990), chapter 10, 'East-West Economic Relations', pp. 305-349.
40. Leonard Geron, *Soviet Foreign Economic Policy under Perestroika* (London, 1990), Appendix 4, p. 109.
41. Hannes Adomeit, 'Gorbachev and German Unification: Revision of Thinking, Realignment of Power', in *Problems of Communism*, July-August 1990, Vol. XXXIX, pp. 1-23.
42. See note 38.
43. See note 37.
44. *Frankfurter Allgemeine*, 'Eine überflüssige Bank', 16 January 1990.
45. British Overseas Development Institute, Briefing Paper, The European Bank for Reconstruction and Development, September 1990, p. 1.
46. *The Economist*, 'A BERD in the hand', 20 January 1990: p. 113 'Initially, the European Commission wanted an affiliate of the existing European Investment Bank to meet the need. But commission officials complain that because the EIB failed to come up with any ideas, the commission had no choice but to back the French idea of a new institution'.
47. British Overseas Development Institute, Briefing Paper, The European Bank for Reconstruction and Development, September 1990.
48. *Financial Times*, 'BERD gets ready to fly', 29 May 1990.
49. J.M.C. Rollo, *The New Eastern Europe: Western Responses* (London, 1990) pp. 128-131.
50. Bimal Ghosh, 'Money can't buy reform', in *European Affairs* 3/90, pp. 99-100.
51. *Bulletin of the European Community*, 12 - 1989, Belgium, January 1990, point 1.1.20.
52. *Ibid.*, point 1.1.14 (iv).

Chapter 4
1. *Bulletin of the European Community*, 1/2-1990, Belgium, May 1990, point 1.2.7.
2. Discours prononcé par monsieur François Mitterrand President de la République devant le Parlement Européen à Strasbourg, 25 octobre 1989, Service de Presse de la Présidence de la République.
3. *Bulletin of the European Community*12 - 1989, Belgium, January 1990, point 1.1.14 (iv).

4. Speech of Mr. François Mitterrand, President of the Republic, at the first session of the conference setting up the European Bank for Reconstruction and Development (Paris, 15 January 1990), Speeches and Statements Sp.St/LON/8/90, French embassy London.
5. *International Herald Tribunhe*, 'Talks Fail to Set Terms for East European Bank', 12 March 1990. Mr. Attali: 'We have opened up the teller's window, the more countries that wish to support the revolutions in Central and Eastern Europe, the better'.
6. *Financial Times*, 'Trade tops Roh agenda in Moscow', 13 December 1990, p. 4. The Soviet Union, traditionally North Korea's principal trade investment partner, is now courting co-operation with South Korea's dynamic economy. For their part South Korean businessmen are hungrily eyeing a potential market and a new source of raw material. Diplomatic relations were established in September 1990.
7. *International Herald Tribune*, 'Israël Seeks to Join European Bank', 29 January 1990.
8. Ibrahim F.I. Shihata, *The European Bank for Reconstruction and Development* (London, 1990), p. 173.
9. *Ibid.*, p. 2.
10. R. Keller & J.H.P. de Vries, De Europese Bank voor Wederopbouw en Herstel: een bank met een missie, in *ESB* 30 May 1990, p. 489.
11. *Bulletin of the European Community* 10 - 1989, Belgium, November 1989, pp. 79-86.
12. *The Economist* 'The BERD struggles to leave the egg', 7 April 1990, p. 70.
13. *International Herald Tribune*, 'Objecting to Moscow Loans', 13 April 1990: 'Two of the leading opponents of the new European Bank for Reconstruction and Development are the Senate Republican leader, Bob Dole of Kansas, and Senator Robert W. Kasten Jr. of Wisconsin, the ranking Republican on the Senate Appropriations Committee'.
14. Robert Marjolin, *Architect of European Unity/Memoirs* 1911-1986 (London, 1989), p. 182.
15. *International Herald Tribune*, 'U.S. Threat on Europe Bank', 16 March 1990. An other article, in the *Financial Times*, 19 March 1990, quotes President Bush: direct financial aid for the Soviet Union was not in America's interest, nor was it needed to 'encourage reform, *perestroika* and *glasnost* in the Soviet Union'. The bank was set up 'to help smaller countries in Eastern Europe who are going down democracy's road'.
16. *The Times*, 'US hard line on aid for Russia', 16 March 1990. In this context an article in the *Financial Times*, 26 March 1990, quotes US Treasury Secretary Brady: 'Let's conjure up together what the headlines will be if we didn't join this. It's kind of a stark position to think us not as a member'.
17. EBRD Agreement, 29 May 1990, Article 5.1, Subscription of shares.
18. Pierre Townsend, 'Europeans worry EBRD has been co-opted by the US', in *Annual Meetings News*, Washington, 23 September 1990, p. 35.
19. Viktor V. Gerashchenko, 'Global Economic Institutions: The Russians are coming', in *European Affairs* 3/90, pp. 55-58.
20. Darell Delamaide, 'Friends in High Places', in *Euromoney* June 1990, pp. 24-30.
21. *The Economist*, 'A BERD in the hand', 20 January 1990, pp. 111-113.

22. British Overseas Development Institute, The European Bank for Reconstruction and Development, Briefing Paper, September 1990, p. 3.

23. European Investment Bank, EIB Information, July 1990 nr. 65, p. 3.

24. EBRD Agreement, 29 May 1990, Article 5.1, Subscription of shares.

25. EBRD Agreement, 29 May 1990, Article 12.1, Limitation on ordinary operations.

26. Comparison of EC countries shares in the capital of the EIB (100% of total) and the EBRD (45% of total) capital: Germany, France, Italy, Britain each 19.127-18.928, Spain 7.031-7.556, Netherlands 5.302-5.511, Belgium 5.302-5.067, Denmark 2.684-2.667, Greece 1.438-1.444, Portugal 0.927-0.933, Ireland 0.671-0.667 and Luxembourg 0.134-0.444.

27. *Frankfurter Allgemeine*, 'Um die "Osteuropa-Bank" wird weiter gestritten', 1 February 1990.

28. Letter from dr. Theo Waigel, German Finance Minister, to Mr. J. Attali dated 17 October 1990: '. . . the two German states have united to form one sovereign state, as a single member of the European Bank for Reconstruction and Development remains bound by the provisions of the Agreement . . . under the name of "Germany". . . . The Federal Republic of Germany does not intend to take up the share of the capital stock subscribed by the former German Democratic Republic . . .'.

29. See Stefan D. Krasner, *Structural Conflict, the Third World against global liberalism* (Berkeley, 1985), pp. 151-164.

30. EBRD Agreement, 29 May 1990, Article 29.1, Voting.

31. Ibrahim F.I. Shihata, *The European Bank for Reconstruction and Development* (London, 1990), p. 90.

32. *Bulletin of the European Community*, 12 -1989, Belgium, January 1990, point 1.1.14 (iv).

33. Speech of Mr. Francois Mitterrand, President of the Republic, at the first session of the conference setting up the European Bank for Reconstruction and Development (Paris, 15 January 1990), Speeches and Statements, Sp.St/LON/8/90, French embassy London.

34. British Overseas Development Institute, Briefing Paper, European Bank for Reconstruction and Development, September 1990, p. 2.

35. Pierre Townsend, 'European worry EBRD has been co-opted by US', in *Annual Meetings News*, Washington, 23 September 1990, p. 35.

36. *The Independent*, 'Attali defines EBRD role', 31 May 1990.

37. Leonard Geron, *Soviet Foreign Economic Policy under Perestroika* (London 1990), p. 102.

38. Viktor V. Gerashchenko, 'Global Economic Institutions: The Russians are coming', in *European Affairs* 3/90, pp. 55-58.

39. *Bulletin of the European Community*, 12/89, Belgium, January 1990, p. 132.

40. *Le Monde*, 'La BERD pourrait commencer ses prêts à l'Est en mars 1991', 11 April 1990.

41. R. Keller & J.H.P. de Vries, 'De Europese Bank voor Wederopbouw en Herstel: een bank met een missie', in *ESB* 30 May 1990, pp. 488-490.

42. *Financial Times*, 'US likely to join bank to aid reform in E Europe', 26 March 1990.

43. For an extensive review of this issue see Ibrahim F.I. Shihata, *The European*

Bank for Reconstruction and Development (London, 1990), pp. 11-19.
44. Graham Hancock, *Lords of poverty*, (Worcester, GB, 1989), pp. 158-159. Hancock estimates the benefits resulting from the UN offices in Vienna at US $100 million a year and in Geneva at US $120 million a year.
45. Darell Delamaide, 'Friends in High Places', in *Euromoney*, June 1990, p. 26.
46. *Le Monde*, 'Le Danemark veut accueillir la banque européenne pour les pays de l'Est', 24 December 1989.
47. *International Herald Tribune*, 'Now London Seeks to Host Europe Bank', 14 February 1990.
48. *Financial Times*, 'London moves up in race to host E Europe bank', 24 April 1990.
49. *The Economist*, 'The BERD struggles to leave the egg', 7 April 1990, p. 70.
50. *International Herald Tribune*, 'Ruding Tipped for Bank Post', 19 January 1990.
51. *International Herald Tribune*, 'Pro-democracy Bank Forgets Its Raison d'Etre', 11 April 1990.
52. *Le Monde*, 'La présidence de la Banque pour l'Est pourrait revenir à M. Jacques Attali', 9 February 1990.
53. *The Independent*, 'UK victory near over bank site', 27 April 1990.
54. *International Herald Tribune*, 'Dutch object as Europe Bank deal is ratified', 21 May 1990. Amsterdam and Copenhagen each won five votes, with the remaining six votes scattered among four other cities. According to the *International Herald Tribune*, 'New Bank Foresees Losses', 19 October 1990, the British government made available an US $15 million subsidy to help pay for the EBRD's headquarters.
55. *International Herald Tribune*, 'Dutch still upset over bank', 28 May 1990. Also *Financial Times*, 'Mitterrand sees wide role for new European bank', 30 May 1990.
56. R. Cohen, *The Theatre of Power/the art of diplomatic signalling* (Essex/England, 1987), p. 157.
57. *The Economist*, 8 December 1990, p. 70.
58. *Financial Times*, 'High-flyer for the EBRD', 4 December 1990, p. 37.

Chapter 5

1. M.A.G. van Meerhaeghe, *International Economic Institutions*, fifth revised edition (Dordrecht, 1987), p. 16.
2. J.M.C. Rollo, *The New Eastern Europe: Western Responses* (London, 1990), pp. 6-12.
3. Chairman's Report on the Agreement establishing the EBRD, Appendix V in Ibrahim F.I. Shihata, *The European Bank for Reconstruction and Development* (London, 1990), p. 169.
4. Stefan D. Krasner, *Structural Conflict: the Third World against global liberalism* (Berkeley, 1985), pp. 151-152.
5. EIB Information, July 1990, nr. 65, p. 5.
6. Chairman's Report on the Agreement establishing the EBRD, Appendix V in Ibrahim F.I. Shihate, *The European Bank for Reconstruction and Development* (London, 1990), p. 177.

7. EBRD Press Release, 17 April 1991.
8. See note 6.

Chapter 6

1. *Financial Times*, 'EBRDetails', 24 July 1990: Mr. P. Pissaloux of the French Ministry of Finance was appointed Chef de Cabinet and Mrs. S. Jay of the British Overseas Administration was appointed Assistent Chef de Cabinet. Both had been a member of the delegation of their respective countries in the constitutive meetings.
2. *International Herald Tribune*, 'Attali says Europe Bank now has full support', 25 October 1990: Quote of Mr. Attali the people of Eastern Europe were 'happy to get rid of bureaucracy, not for us to recreate one'.
3. *Financial Times*, 'Attali's bank plan faces US criticisms', 30 July 1990.
4. *Financial Times*, 'Autocracy and tears at the bank that would free east Europe, 2 August 1990.
5. *International Herald Tribune*, 'Aid Bank for East Europe Faces Stiff Challenge', 27 December 1990.
6. *International Herald Tribune*, 'New bank foresees losses', 19 October 1990.
7. Letter by Mr. Attali to design schools in all member countries, dated 23 October 1990.
8. *International Herald Tribune*, 'East European bank defines investment goals', 31 January 1991.
9. *Financial Times*, 'Euro catch?', 19 September 1990.
10. According to *The Guardian*, 'Attali maps out new Europe', 15 November 1990, Mr. Attali, 'to find a chief economist wrote to Nobel Laureates in Economics and asked them for a shortlist of candidates. He took the one name that appeared on all the lists, John Flemming'.
11. *The Independent*, 'Attali finds his man at last', 7 June 1991.
12. *The Financial Times*, 'European Bank appoints Wall Street man as vice-president', 7 June 1991.
13. *Le Monde*, 'Les députés ratifient l'accord sur la BERD', 24 June 1990 and *Le Monde*, 'Adoptions définitives au Sénat', 30 June 1990.
14. *Financial Times*, 'Euro-bank clears hurdle', 30 March 1991.
15. *International Herald Tribune*, 'Bonn makes credit plea for Soviets', 23 March 1991.
16. *Financial Times*, 'Moscow pressed to build private sector economy', 12 June 1991.
17. *Ibid.*
18. *The Wall Street Journal*, 'EBRD to Help Establish Bank in Soviet Union', 12 June 1991.

Chapter 7

1. M.A.G. van Meerhaeghe, *International Economic Institutions*, fifth revised edition (Dordrecht, 1987), p. 16.
2. *The Economist*, 13 April 1991, pp. 18–19.
3. *Financial Times*, 'BERD gets ready to fly', 29 May 1990.

4. *International Herald Tribune*, 'Poland wins "extraordinary" terms of forgiveness on debt', 16–17 March 1991.
5. EBRD Press Release, 17 April 1991.
6. *Financial Times*, 'Time for a profitable advance on human rights', 21 August 1990.

Index